Nigel J. Lobo is a chef currently living and working in Dubai as a Group Executive Chef. From working stages at Michelin starred restaurants in Spain to some of the best restaurants in the world in Australia and Germany to now running Stars N' Bars-UAE, his experiences set him up for culinary success at a very young age. And it's these experiences that he wants to share with a larger audience, hoping to inspire and guide the next generation of chefs to realize their true hidden potential.

I would like to thank, and dedicate this book, to all my mentors who saw something special in me and believed in me, even when I didn't.

Chefs Jitin Joshi, Bobby Kapoor, Deep Mohan Singh Bajaj, Udayshankar Shenoy, Vikas Vichare, Paco Perez, Mateu Casanas, and Oriol Castro.

I would also like to dedicate this book to all the young, aspiring chefs out there who are passionate about food and want to immerse themselves in the madness that is 'the culinary world'.

Nigel Lobo

INSIGHT

A Comprehensive Guide to Help You Become a Successful Chef in the Culinary World

AUSTIN MACAULEY PUBLISHERS™
LONDON • CAMBRIDGE • NEW YORK • SHARJAH

Copyright © Nigel Lobo 2022

The right of Nigel Lobo to be identified as author of this work has been asserted by the author in accordance with Federal Law No. (7) of UAE, Year 2002, Concerning Copyrights and Neighboring Rights.

All rights reserved. No part of this publication may be reproduced, stored in a retrieval system, or transmitted in any form or by any means, electronic, mechanical, photocopying, recording, or otherwise, without the prior permission of the publishers.

Any person who commits any unauthorized act in relation to this publication may be liable to legal prosecution and civil claims for damages.

This is a work of fiction. Names, characters, businesses, places, events, locales, and incidents are either the products of the author's imagination or used in a fictitious manner. Any resemblance to actual persons, living or dead, or actual events is purely coincidental.

The age group that matches the content of the books has been classified according to the age classification system issued by the National Media Council.

ISBN – 9789948043645 – (Paperback)
ISBN – 9789948043652 – (E-Book)

Application Number: MC-10-01-5923159
Age Classification: E

Printer Name: iPrint Global Ltd
Printer Address: Witchford, England

First Published 2022
AUSTIN MACAULEY PUBLISHERS FZE
Sharjah Publishing City
P.O Box [519201]
Sharjah, UAE
www.austinmacauley.ae
+971 655 95 202

Thank you to my mom, Sheila Lobo, my dad, Norman Lobo, and Psycho-Nicole Lobo. None of this would have been possible without the sacrifices you have all made to make sure that I got all the opportunities I needed to learn, grow, and become the chef I am today. This is for you.

I would also like to thank the entire Andrade family and their families who at various stages in my culinary career were there as support: Cynthia, Sylvie, Saira, and Sonika.

And I can't continue without giving a shout out to Uday Chandran, a great friend, confidant, teammate, and my human diary; I definitely wouldn't have found the right words to tell my story if it wasn't for you.

Introduction

Over the years, much has changed in the gastronomical realm. Technology and a sense of scientific enquiry now go hand in hand with how chefs work and think. Many new ingredients are making their way into our day-to-day diet (2019 can definitely be called the year of *Kale*), while at the same time, we are rediscovering ingredients and flavor profiles that were lost in the annals of history. And with social media becoming deeply ingrained in all areas of our lives, it is also much harder to get away with a mediocre offering be it your dish, your restaurant, or even the behavior of your wait staff. This means, today, it is not just important to cook up great food; the experience you offer to a diner plays as much a role, if not more, in wooing a steady clientele and making your restaurant a success.

However, the biggest change if you ask me is the fact that if young chefs show talent and the drive to stand out, today people are willing to take a chance on them. Me? I got my first big break just before my 24th birthday taking the helm of the kitchen at the Eloquent Elephant at Taj Dubai where I was mentored by Chef Jitin Joshi. A decade ago, this would seem almost impossible.

But as much as things have changed, much remains the same. A strong foundation still remains key to a chef's success in the kitchen. Working your way up in a kitchen is still the best way to inculcate a sense of responsibility, decision-making, and discipline in you. An in-depth understanding of flavor and meticulousness are still the cornerstones of what makes a great chef. And it is this focus on enhancing my skills and knowledge that led me to kitchens across the world. Without these experiences, I'm not sure if I would have had the confidence and self-belief to take over the Eloquent Elephant when the opportunity arose.

Maybe I'm getting a little ahead of myself. Before becoming the Executive Chef & Group Culinary Administrator at the Royal Orchid Hospitality Group, before I took over the kitchen at the Eloquent Elephant, before I even stepped foot into a professional kitchen, I was a young boy living in Dubai, doing what all young boys do; playing football, hanging out with friends and, whiling away time watching TV. And it is during these TV binge sessions, watching chefs on TLC cooking by the beach as they sip wine, that sparked my curiosity for cooking. This was further fed by the books I read, especially '*Alinea*' by Grant Achatz, whose passion inspired me immensely.

All this meant is that when it came time to decide what I would do after high school, there was only one path for me to take—apply to culinary school. Out of the ones I applied to, I chose to enroll myself in the Systematic Training and Education Program (STEP) run by The Oberoi Hotels & Resorts because of their strong focus on the culinary arts. And from here began my journey into this hectic, yet fascinating world.

Posted at the Oberoi Bangalore, I spent the next three years working in various Kitchen Departments, being exposed to every possible kitchen scenario. Where each day offered a new challenge and there was never a dull moment. My responsibilities didn't just strengthen my foundation as a chef; it also gave me a great bird's eye view of the hotel and restaurant business, giving me insights into how other hotel departments such as the front office, food & beverage and housekeeping are run as well. By the time I finished STEP, I had no doubt in my mind that this was my calling.

And my journey at The Oberoi continued. After STEP, I was one of only 50 applicants selected for the Postgraduate Diploma in Kitchen Management offered by the Oberoi Center for Learning and Development. An exclusive program that boasts alumni such as Michelin starred Chef Atul Kochhar of Benares fame and Chef Vivek Singh of the Cinnamon Club; here, I perfected the art of creating reports and presentations, analyzing data, monitoring logistics, and other managerial skills apart from enhancing my cooking techniques.

But the more I learned, the more my thirst for knowledge increased. So, I took off to travel the world and add to what I knew. These travels took me from Germany where I trained at La Vie (Three Michelin Stars) under Chef Thomas Buhner and gained an appreciation for slow cooking. And because I was the tiniest pea in the pod, I got a chance to refresh my basics, learn about stocks and purees from the ground up, and truly opened my eyes to the art of presentation which was nothing short of spectacular there. Then, at Attica in Melbourne (Three Hatted and the then 21st best in the world), I learned how locally grown herbs and shrubs elevate food to a whole new level, learning about the importance of having your own garden, and the uniqueness of wild herbs. And after my last posting with The Oberoi at the Oberoi Udaivillas, my travels took me to Spain, where I trained at Miramar (Two Michelin Stars) and Compartir (from the chef de cuisines of El Bulli), both of which taught me the importance of consistency.

And through it all, I made sure I took part in as many competitions as I could, further honing my skills and technique.

It is these experiences that helped me grow into a chef who, even at 24, could create a distinct gastro pub philosophy for the Eloquent Elephant, train the people under me, and most importantly, live up to the faith put in me by Chef Jitin Joshi. And in the years when I worked there, we received Two Black Hats in the What's on Guide 2015, and won *OK! Magazine* Editors' Choice Award 2016 and Time Out Best Pub Food 2017.

Additionally, I was Runners up for Young Hotelier of The Year at the Leaders in Hospitality Awards, Middle East, 2017 and a semi-finalist at the prestigious San Pellegrino Young Chef of the year in 2018. However, the highlight so far has to be making it to the finals of Cocinando con trufa—Cooking with truffles. Being the youngest contestant and making it to the final ten was a matter of pride in itself. But, making it to the finals and cooking for a jury of thirteen Michelin star chefs whilst representing UAE was the cherry on the top. All this, whilst cooking my finals dish with my assistant who I had only met a day before.

Today, I work with an international chain based in Monaco taking care of their outposts in Dubai and Abu Dhabi as their Group Executive Chef, helping them run and manage their restaurants. Getting here, and planning for beyond, wouldn't have been possible without all my experiences along the way.

And this book is the culmination of those very experiences which I hope will be a great guide for young chefs and restaurateurs who want to enter the profession but don't know where to begin. Because I definitely didn't.

After all, of all those who want to become chefs, only a few ever decide to take it to the next level. From the few, a mere handful might actually make it to the top and experience the success they dreamed of when they started. And even then, it might not turn out the way they expected.

Take me for example. I was mesmerized by the chefs on TV, cooking by the beach with pretty girls on either side. But the closest I get to the beach is seeing it out of my office window while I work on the purchasing plan for the week. The rest of the time, I flit between restaurant to restaurant, fighting fires (figuratively and sometimes literally), providing guidance and making sure everything runs smoothly.

Am I successful? Many would believe so. But for a 15-year-old me, the lack of beaches and pretty girls might not really say "success". And it's this difference between the idea of success in the culinary world and what success actually looks like that creates a disconnect for many who get into this industry. Which, sooner or later, makes them feel jaded and unhappy.

That's why I decided to sit down and write down my experiences. To help young chefs who are serious about pursuing a career in the kitchen and give a clearer idea to those who are still not sure if this is the right path for them. Everything to ensure that before you start your journey down this road, you are equipped with the knowledge and conviction you need to blaze your own trail to the top.

After all, as I mentioned, a lot has changed. And I believe it is time for the younger generation to take the reins and prove that a young chef can fill big shoes. All they need is a nudge in the right direction, which I hope this book will provide, helping hone young minds seeking adventure in the modern world of cuisine, while also helping them adapt to this ever-changing and ever-evolving industry.

Chapter 1:
History of Chefs and Restaurants

Before we dive into the culinary world of today, I believe it is important to look back in time and trace the journey of food in our lives and how it has become such an important cornerstone of our culture and society. Because it is only when you understand the past that you can transform the future, right?

So, are you ready to dive in?

Then let's get right to it…

The Origins of Food

I'm sure you'll all agree when I say the history of our evolution is deeply entwined with the history of food. It is widely believed that early man was a meat-eater, sustaining himself and his tribe with raw meat procured through hunting wild game that lived around them. But the discovery of fire changed everything.

First, raw meat gave way to cooked meat. Then came farming, which led our ancestors to leave behind their life of hunting and gathering and settle down in what would become precursors to modern-day towns and villages. Here, they raised livestock, worked, lived, and whatever they lacked, they bartered for with their neighbors. When people had leftover food, they probably decided to barter or sell them for higher valued goods. This, I believe, is the earliest example of what we call a restaurant today.

From here, as the world became smaller and smaller due to the advent of exploration and the opening of new trade routes, people were exposed to unknown ingredients and newer methods of cooking. Talented chefs were highly sought after by royal families, for whom they cooked with exotic ingredients sourced from newly discovered lands using highly guarded recipes. And as their armies marched across continents for months and years to conquer and expand the kingdom, there was a need to preserve food and meats so they would last for longer. So food was fermented, salted, dried everything to ensure that the marching army could sustain their energy through hostile terrains.

While many of these recipes and techniques have been lost in the sands of time, we do know that the former trade center and bustling metropolis of then Constantinople had cafes where educated people came to meet, share ideas, debate, plan, and drink. They would dine on 'snacks' and drink various brews. Many of these cafes served coffee, a stimulating drink and hence the word "cafe". Cafes in France also sold brandy, sweetened wines, and liqueurs in addition to coffee. In fact, the first modern-type cafe is believed to be Cafe Procope which opened in 1696.

However, many credit a Frenchman, Monsieur A. Boulanger, with creating an establishment that most closely resembles the restaurants of today. By this, I mean a sheltered structure which one could visit during a certain period of the day, sit down and order a meal that was cooked on-premises.

According to *Larousse Gastronomique*, the French culinary book, Boulanger set up an establishment in Paris whose sign proclaimed, "*Boulanger débite des restaurants divins*," or "Boulanger sells restoratives fit for the gods." At the time, "restaurant" meant "restorative" and described the meat-based consommé that was sold at these establishments. The word came from the French word "*restaurer*", which means "to restore [life]". The broth was indeed thought to restore strength to people who were feeling unwell and is the precursor to the consommé that many enjoy today.

And from here sprang other similar establishments, all offering restorative broths that were nutritious and rejuvenated people instantly. It's these that lay the foundation for all the modern-day cafes or restaurants. And the rest, as they say, is history!

The Chef's Hierarchy

Today, when you enter a professional kitchen, it is quite easy to see a positional hierarchy system in place that ensures the kitchen functions smoothly and error-free. But the actual basis for this hierarchy goes all the way back to the late 19th century when Georges-Auguste Escoffier developed the brigade system in London's prestigious Savoy Hotel. Here, for maximum efficiency, he organized the kitchen into a strict hierarchy of authority, responsibility and function, and that is still the system that we follow today in most restaurants.

In a typical modern kitchen, the executive chef will coordinate the kitchen activities, manage costs, and direct the efforts of everyone else. The sous chef is in charge of ensuring that the food is prepared, portioned, and presented to the executive chef's standards. And the line cooks run the stations and prepare menu items, where they are aided by assistants and apprentices.

However, the size and structure of the kitchen hierarchy vary depending on the cuisine offered by the restaurant and its size. It is unlikely that a smaller kitchen will have a dedicated person for every section, but a bigger kitchen may have two, three, or even more. But before you enter the culinary world, it is important that you know the kitchen hierarchy in its entirety so you can understand how the kitchen works.

So what exactly is the hierarchy in a professional kitchen? Here, I will talk about the 8 most typical roles and their function in the modern kitchen.

1. Executive Chef:

Sitting at the top of the kitchen's hierarchy, the Executive Chef's primary role is mostly managerial, not just for one kitchen, but for an entire group of kitchens under one brand or banner. They tend to manage kitchens at multiple outlets, handling the bigger picture and are usually not directly involved in cooking on a day-to-day basis.

2. Chef de Cuisine or Head Chef:

French for Head Chef, the Chef de Cuisine is in charge of the managerial duties of the kitchen they run. They are responsible for supervising and managing staff in the kitchen, controlling costs, and purchasing, liaising with the restaurant manager, creating new menus and more.

3. Sous Chef or Deputy Chef:

While the Sous Chef may share a lot of the same responsibilities as the Head Chef, they are a lot more involved in the day-to-day operations in the kitchen. They are the ones who ensure every dish meets the

Executive or Head Chef's standards before it is sent out to the restaurant's patrons.

4. Chef de Partie or Station Chef

Now we come to the roles that actually keep the kitchen ticking day-to-day. As the Station Chef, you are responsible for one particular section of the kitchen. This means, for different sections, there are different Station Chefs, the roles of whom we can widely classify to include the following:

- Saute Chef or Saucier: Sauteeing foods and creating sauces and gravies to accompany the dishes.
- Boucher: Preparing meat and poultry before it is delivered to the respective stations.
- Poissonnier: Preparing fish and seafood before it is delivered to the respective stations.
- Rotisseur: Roasting meats and creating appropriate sauces.
- Friturier: Preparing fried food items.
- Grillardin: Responsible for everything that is grilled.
- Garde Manger: Preparing cold dishes, such as salads.
- Patissier: Preparing all things pasty, baked goods and desserts.
- Chef de Tournant: Responsible for filling in as and when needed at different stations.
- Entremetier: Preparing vegetables,

soups, starches and eggs.

5. Commis Chef or Junior Chef

The Junior Chef is generally someone who has either recently completed their formal kitchen training or is still in the process of completing it. So they work under the Station Chef to learn the ins and outs of a particular station.

6. Kitchen Porter

The ones least likely to have formal training, but who I believe to be the most crucial part of the kitchen, the Kitchen Porter assists with basic tasks such as food preparation and cleaning.

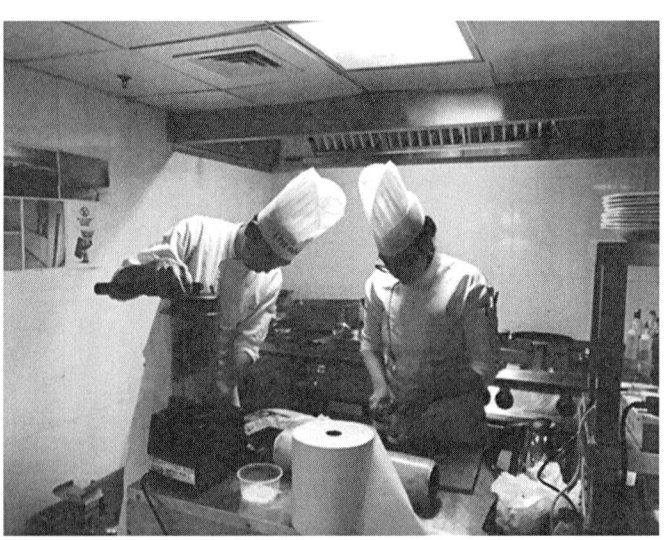

7. Escuelerie or Dishwasher

As evident by the name, the Escuelerie is responsible for washing anything that was used in the kitchen to prep or process.

8. Aboyeur or Waiter/Waitress

Working in the front end of the restaurant, the waiters and waitresses take the customers' orders, communicate the order to the kitchen and ensure that the overall restaurant experience of the customer is satisfactory.

The Chef's Uniform

As a Chef, I think the proudest moment of my life was when I was handed my chef whites. I still remember it as clearly as if it was yesterday. The pride of getting measured, achieving the aim of getting my own chef coat with navy blue piping, to be among the few elite artists in the kitchen. The exhilarating feeling of having your name embroidered on it for the first time and carrying it with pride is something words cannot describe. It was a rush to put it on and finally feel a sense of achievement and acceptance in such a tightly knit industry that is filled with talent and creativity. And with it came the confidence in my own abilities so I could learn and improve my skills in the kitchen. The funny thing is that as I grew and matured in the kitchen, I now want my whites as plain as possible.

But where did it all begin? To trace the origin of the chef's uniform, we need to travel all the way back to 1822, when French artist Marie-Antoine Careme created a sketch called "Le Maître d'Hôtel Français". In that portrait, she depicted two French chefs wearing a uniform that would not be out of place in one of today's kitchens: chef's hat or toque, trousers, a double-breasted jacket, and an apron. And soon, it was the vogue across restaurants in France.

And while many modern chefs may wear a less formal version, it is easy to see how many of the pieces are still a part of their attire. This means when you don the chef's uniform, you are continuing a centuries-old tradition, and each element plays an important role in keeping you safe and comfortable in the kitchen environment.

So, what exactly is included in a chef's uniform? I'm glad you asked.

1. The Toque or Chef's Hat

The Toque has to be the most recognizable piece of apparel in a chef's uniform. After all, it's hard to imagine a chef and not automatically think of the tall, rounded and pleated chef's hat. And while it may have been used historically to mark the rank and importance of a chef in the kitchen, today it serves a more practical purpose to keep hair from falling into the dish and absorb sweat that is guaranteed to accumulate on the brow in the hot and humid kitchen conditions.

2. Double-breasted Jacket

The chef's double-breasted jacket is designed primarily keeping functionality in mind. Made from heavy cotton, it ensures breathability while also protecting the chef from heat and hot spills. Being double-breasted provides additional protection against burns and spills, while also allowing for easy and quick removal in case of an accident. Another advantage of the double-breasted design is it helps chefs hide spills during work hours, allowing them to look more presentable and clean no matter how crazy the kitchen gets.

3. **Pants**

Obviously, chefs wear pants. We all do. However, a pair of chef's pants need to follow very specific guidelines. They should be dark-colored so stains and spills are easily hidden. Many are also patterned, which further hides these stains. But most importantly, they should be loose so the chef can move around the kitchen unhindered.

4. **Apron**

A vast majority of chefs wear an apron as added protection against heat, flames, and spillage. The apron is generally made of heavy-duty, flame-retardant material, and may have pockets in which chefs can store their tools.

5. **Shoes**

A chef may be on their feet for 10-12 hours, or even more, depending on their responsibilities. This means, wearing well-fitting shoes that are comfortable is a priority. They should also have a good grip to minimize the risk of slips and falls. Finally, they need to be sturdy to protect the chef against spillage of hot liquids or falling pots and vessels.

I hope you now have a better idea of the uniform and the role that each piece plays.

What's that? Why do chefs wear white?

I can't believe I forgot that.

While the color itself is a symbol of cleanliness and perfection, there are two main practical reasons why chefs wear white.

First, the color is great at reflecting heat, which offers the chef additional protection in the kitchen.

Second, even though white shows stains quickly, it can be bleached clean easily, saving time and effort.

And now that we've covered all your questions, let's move on.

The Michelin Rating System

Everyone knows Gordon Ramsay. The gruff, no-nonsense chef is the epitome of professionalism and order. Now, I would like you to imagine what it would take to reduce such a strong, world-renowned chef to tears.

If you said the loss of two Michelin Stars, you got it right.

In 2015, Gordon Ramsay's New York restaurant, the London, lost two Michelin Stars. And to understand why it had such a deep effect on him, I think it is important to understand the origins of this distinguished culinary award and what it represents.

So what exactly are Michelin Stars?

For every great chef, the chase is the same. If you don't have a Michelin Star, you're trying your hardest to get one. And for those who already have one, you can't help but strive to get another. A Michelin Star is a badge of honor that symbolizes that the chef has succeeded at the highest level. Two Michelin Stars propel you to the higher echelons of the culinary arts, and getting reservations for the few restaurants that hold Three Michelin Stars is next to impossible, even for most VIPs.

How did it begin? And how did it achieve such reverence?

The origin of Michelin Stars can be traced back to 1900 in France, where they were originally a feature of the

Michelin Guide books published by the founders of the Michelin tire company Andre and Edouard Michelin.

At that time, driving was a new phenomenon and the Michelin brothers were trying to find ways to get people to travel in cars more, and hence, buy more tires. And with the book, the brothers provided a wealth of information for tourists, including where to stop for the best meals and the best places to stay.

As history shows, traveling in cars picked up immensely, and by the time the 1920s rolled around, the dining element of the books surpassed every other section in terms of demand and readership. That's when Michelin set up a team of inspectors whose only job was to visit restaurants and rate them, anonymously. The rating system, referred to as Michelin Stars, is still in place today.

1. Star denotes a very good restaurant in its category.
2. Stars denote a restaurant with excellent cooking that's worth a detour.
3. Stars denote a restaurant that's worth a special journey.

Today, Michelin Stars are offered to only a selected group of restaurants globally for their outstanding quality. In fact, there are only 137 restaurants across the world with 3 Michelin Stars as of 2019.

And this leads us to how Michelin Stars ended up earning such reverence. Even though there is a growing trend around the world to reject Michelin Stars (and the pressures that come with earning and holding on to them), some leading chefs and restaurateurs believe it is the only authentic rating system around.

That's because Michelin inspectors are one of the few that still remain anonymous while visiting a restaurant to rate it. This means they receive no red-carpet treatment and extra attention from the kitchen or the front staff, and the inspectors get to enjoy the same experience that a casual diner would.

At the same time, because of the high standards required across the restaurant to earn a Michelin Star, many believe it forces both the chef and restaurateur to pay even closer attention to their craft.

So while the jury may still be out on whether the Michelin Stars have a positive or negative influence on restaurants and chefs, its impact on the culinary landscape cannot be ignored. The entire world still eagerly anticipates the release of the Guide's new issue every year. And it is still considered a reliable source of information for diners who want an exceptional dining experience.

Personally, I believe that my experiences working at Michelin starred restaurants under chefs who know what it means and takes to earn one has truly impacted how I look not just at cooking the style, the ingredients, the presentation but also at every other facet of running a restaurant that affects the diner's experience.

"Michelin madness", as it is commonly known in the industry, is the drive for perfection. It is how chefs and service professionals dedicate their lives to the craft and create memories for their guests and patrons. You get to learn so much as the whole team is striving for perfection. Service has to be seamless and the food has to be perfect. How do you achieve and maintain such high standards?

It differs from restaurant to restaurant and the vision of the chef. Getting the right produce and cooking according to seasons makes it easier. Standardization of everything can be one. In La Vie, even the water and vegetables in stock were measured. We used to forage just enough for the diners at Attica per day. So, if we had sixty reservations, we used to pluck exactly 61 herbs of the same size for that service.

Miramar was all about perfection and detail. It used to take four recipes to make an amuse bouche. The one thing that stood out in all these restaurants is the passion for the craft and how people have to be focused and consistent on a daily basis.

Now that we're done with the boring stuff, it's time to move on to what you're really here for; to find out how you can become a chef and what it takes to start and run a successful restaurant of your own.

I can't wait to jump right in, and I'm sure neither can you.

So hold on to your toques and let's go for a ride!

Chapter 2: Cuisine

Quick How many different types of cuisine can you name without thinking.

Three? Five? Ten?

No matter how many cuisines you can remember off the top of your head, I think I can safely say that there are many more of which you're barely aware of.

For every well-known cuisine like French there is the magic of Polynesian cuisine of which many are unaware. And what many people club together as "Asian cuisine", is, in fact, an amalgamation of vastly different cuisines from the various regions of Asia. Influences on Vietnamese cuisine are drastically different from those in Thai cuisine. These, in turn, are completely different from Indian cuisine, which would also be a part of "Asian cuisine", India being a part of the Asian subcontinent.

The ingredients used, styles of cooking, the carbohydrates used, they all differ from country to country and even region to region within a country that is vast enough. A country like China boasts a vast variety of cuisines, each specific to and carrying a style unique to that particular province. Sometimes even the utensils used to prepare dishes may vary from region to region as well.

European cuisine similarly differs distinctly from each other within countries in Europe. Having said that, due to the formalization of the kitchen hierarchy, systems and French cuisine, many of the popular dishes follow the study and basis of modern French cooking. The methodology defined in the French system allows for a scientific and systematic approach to food preparation. But with a bigger focus on going back to the roots and cooking with ingredients indigenous to particular European countries, modern European cuisine is similarly distinguishing itself within the region.

Then we come to the techniques. Modern technology now allows us to do so much more than what was possible even five years ago. You can extract essences, convert flavors into sprays, transform the texture of ingredients completely, and if you're a fan of Heston Blumenthal, you know that you can completely fool the senses with the right equipment and techniques.

So what does this mean for you as someone who is just starting off as a chef? As the world becomes a smaller and smaller place, it has become much easier to get access to the cornucopia of ingredients the world produces. This means you can now use ingredients native to Australia (like Kangaroo) to create a German dish like a schnitzel. You are not only limited by your imagination in terms of what you can and cannot do when it comes to mixing different styles and ingredients from different cuisines together. At the same time, it is also easier to expand your knowledge of various cuisines, with enough tools and information available online that you could spend decades going through them all.

Now, for me exploring different cuisines, their ingredients, the techniques of cooking, helps me become a more well-rounded chef. However, this needs a deep understanding of the cuisines from which you're taking inspiration. And as someone who is just starting off, I'm here to help you get a deeper understanding of some of the most popular cuisines from around the world.

Cuisines of the World
1. Mexico

While what we call Mexican cuisine has existed for centuries from the time of the Mayans, it has taken the world by storm over the last decade. Today, you will find at least one Mexican restaurant in every major city center, sometimes authentic, sometimes modified to fit the palate of the people who live there.

One of the biggest reasons Mexican cuisines has caught on so much is because it has a little bit of everything: the zestiness of Greek salads, the tanginess of Indian curries, the freshness and heat of Thai food. Another reason is the fact that most of the ingredients used in the cuisine are highly nutritious, especially so because they are mostly used fresh and uncooked.

Dishes you need to try:

Mole – A sauce that is as old as time, made with chili peppers, spices, and chocolate.

Tamales – Masa cooked in a leaf wrapping, the way the ancient Mayans used to do it

A technique you need to learn:

Desflemar – Mexican cuisine uses a lot of chilies. However, if you want to retain the flavor of chilies while neutralizing the hotness, the Desflemar technique is what you need to know. Simply dip the chilies in water and vinegar or salt, and the heat is drawn out, leaving you with chilies that are more flavorful than hot.

2. Thailand

Thai cuisine is heavily influenced by cuisines from nearby countries, such as China, Malaysia, and Indonesia, as well as a royal culinary tradition that dates back to when the country was first formed. All these influences mean that Thai cuisine is the best of many worlds, bringing together flavors from around the region and amalgamating it into dishes that will leave you licking your lips.

Complex and intense, Thai cuisine fits every single flavor onto one dish be it spicy, tangy, sweet, or sour. At the same time, there is also a heavy focus on textures: the chew, the crunchy, the melt-in-your-mouth. This is because every dish is a symphony of many different herbs and spices, coming together in perfect harmony to create the unmistakable Thai flavor. Just open a Thai cookbook and you'll find that most dishes have ingredient lists that go on for a couple of pages.

Dishes you need to try

Massaman Curry – A Thai curry with its roots in the Islamic heritage of Thailand, this dish tops most "must try" lists in Thai cuisine.

Som Tam – A simple, green papaya salad, its sour, spicy, sweet and salty flavors are the perfect representation of Thailand and their cuisine.

A technique you need to learn:

Steaming – A lot of Thai dishes are prepared by steaming the ingredients in leaves, especially banana leaves. This ensures that direct heat is not applied to whatever you're cooking, allowing for perfect cooking temperatures and great results. This is especially useful when you're preparing fish and seafood dishes.

3. India

Being from India, this is a cuisine that is very close to my heart. Or should I say there are various Indian cuisines that are close to my heart? My family comes from Mangalore, a city in the southern part of India. So needless to say, I grew up loving the many South Indian dishes my mom used to make. As I traveled around India during my STEP and OCLD,

I discovered a love for the way South-East Asian influences have seeped into the cuisine found in the regions northeast of India. And let's not forget North Indian food, the first type of Indian cuisine that most people are exposed to.

As a whole, Indian cuisine places an emphasis on the usage of spices, be it vegetarian or non-vegetarian dishes, putting big and impactful flavors front and center. And because a large part of the Indian population is vegetarian, those who don't eat meat will still find plenty of delicious options to dig into when they try Indian cuisine.

With such a huge variety in cuisines from region to region, it is little surprise that a week or even a month is not enough to explore the length and breadth of what the country has to offer in terms of cuisine. But if you had to start somewhere, I'd suggest you start down south and make your way up. You won't regret it.

Dishes you need to try:
Neer Dosa – A light and melt-in-your-mouth rice pancake, this is the perfect accompaniment to the spicy and tangy curries from the Mangalore region.

Biryani – Hearty and wholesome, biryani is a dish made with rice and meat or vegetables, cooked over a period of time in an earthenware pot until the spices and flavors meld together in perfect harmony.

A technique you need to learn:
Tandoor – Typically, a tandoor is a cylinder made of clay which lets heat escape only from the top. Meat, bread and vegetables are lowered into the enclosure and cooked in high

heat (up to 500 degrees Fahrenheit), sealing in the flavors to create succulent dishes and soft bread.

4. Japan

The Japanese are known for their precision and dedication to perfection. And Japanese cuisine is no different. Whether you choose a lavish multicourse Kaiseki meal or a simple bowl of ramen with vegetables, everything is served with a sense of pride and an emphasis on freshness and nutrition.

The food culture in Japan is varied. There are sushi bars with conveyor belts, allowing you to choose what you like as the dish passes you by. There are late-night ramen restaurants that feed large hordes of hungry customers into the early morning hours. And then there are a plethora of supermarkets and dispensers that provide you with everything from noodles to fresh lobster, whenever you want. It is impossible to choose something to eat in Japan that you won't enjoy.

Dishes you need to try:

Miso Soup – A simple bowl of soup, this single dish perfectly showcases the simplicity and fundamental flavors of Japanese cuisine.

Tempura – The art of Japanese deep-frying, tempura utilizes a thin batter that keeps dishes non-greasy and light, making it different from the deep-fried dishes you're normally used to.

A technique you need to learn:

Mushimono – The Japanese technique of steaming, it allows you to seal in flavors and nutritional value of the ingredients, without the fear of overcooking.

5. Spain

In a country where the culture revolves around eating and spending time with friends and family, it is no surprise that the Spanish are incredibly passionate about their cuisine. They munch on little things all day, with the bigger meals becoming hour-long events where you spend time leisurely going through feasts that are generally staples of such meals.

Influences of the Moorish era, along with staples from various regions across Spain, has led to the creation of a unique culinary delight that you need to dive deep into to explore and experience.

Dishes you need to try:

Jamon Iberico – Cured ham hock that is carved into thin slices, the Jamon Iberico carries flavors unlike any other cured meat.

Gazpacho – Almost a liquid salad, Gazpacho is a refreshing start to any meal, energizing you to sit up and take notice of everything else that lands on your table.

6. China

One of the most food-obsessed cultures in the world, the Chinese are some of the bravest explorers of food around. But they don't just cook and eat anything, they also make sure it smells and tastes delicious.

When in China, you will constantly be asking yourself if you can really eat that. But eat that you will, and maybe even ask for seconds when you realize how truly delicious anything can be made when cooked the right way. At the same time, the various regions of China have such vastly different cuisines, you would be hard-pressed to believe that they are all part of the same country.

Dishes you must try:

Dim sums – Ubiquitous with Chinese cuisine, dim sums come in a variety of shapes with an even larger variety of fillings all wrapped up in a simple rice flour bundle.

Peking duck – A wonder of culinary excellence, every part of this dish is mouth-watering.

A technique you should learn:

Stir Fry – One of the most common techniques used in Chinese cooking, this method uses a wok on high heat to cook ingredients quickly which is a skill in itself. But remember, it is important to keep in mind different cooking times of different ingredients and add them in order accordingly.

These are just some of the many cuisines from around the world that inspire me. I suggest that you take some time off and explore different countries and their cuisines to get a deeper understanding of the ingredients and techniques they use. You might not work with the exact same cuisine, but it will better develop your cooking skills, making you a better chef.

I remember my trip to Australia, where I had the opportunity of a lifetime to stage at Attica, the then 43rd best restaurant in the world. Here, I saw all the efforts and dedication that goes into using sustainable and local products to create modern Australian cuisine that showcases the best the region has to offer. Only the exact amount of ingredients were sourced, including herbs. So when we had 60 plates to be served which needed 60 fronds of herbs, we would pluck only 61 from the garden. And that is what really stuck with me the emphasis on optimally utilizing everything we had around us. Even today, I ensure that all my restaurants keep a keen eye on the ingredients we use, and how much of it we use.

Most of these cuisines have evolved over time as the world becomes smaller and smaller. While a lot of chefs still focus on bringing the best traditional dishes from their cuisine to a worldwide audience, some chefs are working towards transforming these dishes and bringing them to the modern world. This wind of change has spread across Europe, leading to a rise in Modern European cuisine that is taking the culinary world by storm.

What is Modern European cuisine?

The fundamentals of modern European cuisine are more about the themes and associations than they are about hard and fast rules of cooking. As the gastronomic world changes, more and more chefs are placing an emphasis on experimenting with techniques and ideas from different countries, while sourcing ingredients local to their region.

It is this trend that has led to the rise of modern European cuisine, which is a shift towards a more relaxed and less structured attitude towards ingredient combinations and how dishes are prepared.

Such is the fluidity of this cuisine that it is hard to really nail down what makes it what it is. You could point to the adoption of Mediterranean cooking styles involving grilling and roasting, as well as ingredients such as olive oil, fresh garlic and herbs. Or taking classical dishes and reimaging them with exotic ingredients. But what really sets modern European cuisine apart is also what makes it hard to define because it is constantly changing and evolving as chefs experiment with new ingredients and cooking techniques. And it is by experimentation and mixing different styles from different countries that has given rise to this new era of European cooking.

Now that we've taken a little trip around the world exploring different countries and what sets their cuisine apart from the rest, I want to share some of my favorite recipes with you. These aren't just great dishes you can make for your friends and family. They also involve certain techniques and skills that I'm sure will be of help to you as you work towards becoming a professional chef.

Now before we jump into the next section, there is one last thing I want to talk to you about Gastronomy. It is a word you'll hear being thrown around a lot these days, used to define everything from bespoke fine dining experiences to chemical manipulation of ingredients to create something completely new be it in terms of flavor, texture, or scent.

But what exactly is gastronomy?

To put it simply, gastronomy is the relationship between us, our food and the world we live in. It involves the science of human digestion, a study of cultures, as well as the history of ingredients and cooking techniques.

And it has been around ever since humans evolved to question what we were eating and why. So fueled by human curiosity, the early cooks strived to make food taste better, provide more energy, and even imbibe healing properties into what they prepared. But it wasn't till the 1800s that it developed into an actual field of science. Chefs were now more focused on creating the best experience for diners, where all the senses were brought into play. And it goes without saying, that while the rest of the world has caught on, the French were first to claim the title and the field as their very own.

Today, chefs are transforming the landscape of the culinary world with their experiments in gastronomy. All you need to see is the work of someone like Heston Blumenthal and it is easy to see the unfettered and unlimited potential that a focus on gastronomy offers.

While a culinary career is the best way to explore the world of gastronomy and all that it offers, there are careers beyond the kitchen that also have a base in gastronomy.

Some of these include:

Food scientist
Food scientists study the deterioration and processing of food, looking for new sources of nutrition and discovering

new methods and techniques to make processed food delicious, safe and healthy.

Health and Nutrition

Understanding the basic nutritional make-up of an ingredient and the best way to prepare it to preserve all the benefits it has to offer form the crux of any Health and Nutrition career. Additionally, you will need to know how different foods interact with each other, and specific body types, and which foods will best help a certain individual meet their health and nutrition goals.

Food Manufacturing

As the world becomes smaller and smaller, the demand for food manufacturing has shot through the roof. However, manufacturing on a large scale does not mean nutrition should be ignored. That's why gastronomy is used to not just create new food offerings for the public, but also ensure minimal loss of benefits in such industries.

At the end of it, I would like to say that you don't really need to work in the food industry to be a true gastronomer. What you do need is a passion for food and culture, as well as a curiosity for the world at large.

Great attributes for a successful chef, if you have these, I would say you're well on your way to becoming a gastronomer already.

Chapter 3: Education

First up, let's address what I think would be the most burning question in your mind: do I need formal education to get started in the kitchen?

Simple answer? No, you don't.

But will it help?

Absolutely!

When I was figuring out how to get started on my journey as a chef, I spent a lot of time pondering over this dilemma.

Do I jump right in and start at a restaurant, learning as I go?

Or do I take time to hone my basics and really understand what goes on in a kitchen?

While there is no right or wrong path to take as you journey towards your dream of working in a professional kitchen, having a formal education can definitely give you a leg up.

Yes, it might take you a little longer to climb up the kitchen ladder. But this is an industry where you can peak at 30, 40, or even 50. So do you really waste those extra years that you spend honing your skills? I don't think so. In fact, it might actually help you on your way forward in a lot of ways.

- First, and the most obvious, you'll have the answers to a lot of questions you have.
- Second, you'll get to learn and practice in a relatively stress-free environment.
- Third, and most importantly, many institutions provide campus placements, which could be of immense help while you're starting out.

For me, it was obvious from the start that I wanted to join a culinary institute, and so began my research into my options in India and how I could go about getting started. First came my interview for The Oberoi Centre of Learning and Development (OCLD). Turning up one Friday early morning, I waited in line with all the other aspirants. However, I was confident. I had a whole speech prepared for why I deserved a place in the institute, what cooking meant to me and why I wanted to pursue a career in the culinary world. It was short, but to the point. But to my surprise, I seemed to be the only one with any type of speech ready. Everyone else introduced themselves casually, but here I was with a formal speech. And once I spoke and sat down, I somehow knew I had gotten in that my journey was about to begin.

And get in, I did. I was ecstatic as I rushed to my aunt at whose home, I was staying during the interview process to tell her the great news I had been selected for STEP. She was happy for me, but wanted me to still give all the other interviews we had lined up, including the one for IHM that was coming up. But I was dead against it, and I stood my ground. My aunt, being my aunt, also wouldn't back down. And that's how I ended up traveling all over Mumbai alone the next week, trying to find the location for my Taj Aurangabad interview. Somehow, I did find the place, and would you know it, I got through there as well. As much as my aunt hated to admit it, my confidence was pretty well-founded, and she had to agree with the fact that I knew what I wanted and what I wanted to do.

After my entire experience at STEP, I can look back and say that I have no regrets at my choice. Joining the culinary school was one of the best decisions I made, giving me the chance to really learn and grow, making me the chef that I am today.

Sounds good, doesn't it? But before you start calling all the culinary institutes in a 50 miles radius, there are a few things you need to know if you decide to pursue formal education before entering the kitchen.

The most important is that even after finishing a course, any course that formally prepares you to work in the kitchen, you will still end up starting from the very bottom. Yes, from the bottom, just like every other apprentice! Plus, just like every other apprentice, you will be thrust right into the heat and madness that is a professional kitchen.

And trust me when I say that no amount of formal education will help prepare you for the chaos that is service time. I remember my first month in a professional kitchen. And this is after finishing both STEP and OCLD. A new chef had joined the continental kitchen who took great interest in helping me learn and improve my craft, which meant he would use his breaks, and any time we were hanging out together, to teach me new recipes and techniques. During a not-so-busy day, he asked me if I remembered the recipe for a club sandwich. I told him I did, and so, he asked me to put one together.

First, cook the chicken as it takes the longest time to season, grill, and put it in the oven. Done. Second, break an egg and make an omelet. Easy. I pick up an egg from under the counter, whack it with a spoon, but it doesn't break. I take another one, the same thing happens. And again with the next. That's when the chef came up from behind me and asked me a question that made me turn bright red with embarrassment. Do you really expect to make an omelet out of a hard-boiled egg?"

So you see, education is only half the battle. Experience is what really helps you learn how to use all the knowledge you have accumulated.

When you look at it, whether you get a formal education or not, you pretty much start at the same place, get the same experience, and maybe even grow at the same pace. Where you do get a leg up is if the institution you apply to offers placements after your course which would make it relatively easier to get into the industry once you're done learning.

And of course, a formal education will help get your basics right. After all, that's the most important foundation for a chef, isn't it?

There are many institutions around the world that offer specialized courses that are tailored to prepare you for a life in the kitchen. And many of them require you to work at their affiliated restaurant and gain experience simultaneously giving you the best of both worlds. Keep in mind that such courses are mostly offered by larger hotels rather than individual restaurants.

International Institutes

1. Culinary Institute of America (CIA)

The Culinary Institute of America is one of the world's premier culinary colleges with campuses in New York, California and Texas, as well as one in Singapore. Established in 1946, today they have more than 50,000 alumni, each of whom has had the opportunity to learn from educators who have excelled in the food world and earned academic accolades.

The institute offers a wide range of courses, from bachelor's degrees in applied food sciences and culinary science, as well as associated degrees in culinary arts and baking and pastry arts, to name a few.

They also offer students the opportunity to take internships, in addition to working in their own public restaurants, ensuring that you get the chance to acquire real-world skills. Additionally, they offer culinary immersion experiences, allowing you to completely focus on your region and cuisine of choice.

Notable Alumni: Anthony Bourdain, Grant Achatz, Jerome Bocuse, and Charlie Palmer

2. Ecole hôtelière de Lausanne (EHL)

Founded by Jacques Tschumi as a place to train professional hotel staff, Ecole hôtelière de Lausanne opened doors to its first class all the way back in 1893. Today, they have a network of over 25,000 alumni globally, and they continue to train culinary leaders of tomorrow.

They offer shorter programs such as a Culinary & Restaurant Management Certificate, or longer programs such as Bachelor's in Hospitality Management and Master's in Wine & Hospitality Management or Global Hospitality Business, to name a few.

Notable Alumni: Reto Wittwer, Craig Claiborne, and George Plassat.

3. Le Cordon Bleu

This is one that I'm sure all of you know. One of the most prestigious and respected culinary institutes in the world, Le Cordon Bleu was founded in 1895 by Marthe Distel in Paris, journalist and publisher of La Cuisiniere Cordon Bleu magazine.

But today, you don't need to go all the way to Paris to learn from Le Cordon Bleu Master Chefs, the majority of whom come from Michelin-starred restaurants. They now have a presence in 20 countries with 35 international schools to choose from.

They offer a range of programs, from the culinary arts and wine and to management and hospitality. But the most prestigious, and intensive (be warned), is the Grand Diplome. This is a comprehensive program in the classical French technique, that covers both Diplome de Patisserie and Diplôme de Cuisine, giving you an in-depth view into everything you'll need to know.

Notable Alumni: Julia Child, Gaston Acurio, Yotam Ottolenghi, and Giada De Laurentiis.

4. Culinary Institute Lenotre

The Culinary Institute Lenotre may not have the decades-old renown of some of the previous institutes mentioned, but they are still one of the premier culinary schools in the USA. Located in Houston, Texas, what sets them apart is the fact that they welcome students of all ages and from every background, as well as professionals of all levels.

For someone like you who wants to train for a career in the kitchen, they offer a range of programs. These include both diplomas and associate degrees in Culinary Arts and Baking and Pastry Arts, as well as several other Elective Options.

And if you're looking for some hands-on training, Le Bistro located inside the Culinary Institute Lenotre is where you will get the chance to hone your skills while cooking for real guests.

Notable Alumni: Drew Rogers, Sandia Horng, and Michael Jones.

5. Leiths School of Food and Wine

Leiths School of Food and Wine is one of the premier culinary institutes in London. And when they boast teachers such as the Michelin-starred Atul Kochhar and Angela Malik, it is quite obvious why students rush to their courses.

They offer a range of courses to prepare you for a career in cooking, including Three and Two Term Diplomas in Food and Wine, varying levels of Certification in Food and Wine, and Accreditations in Nutrition, to name a few.

Notable Alumni: Angela Malik, Esther Clark, Gizzi Erskine, and Tomek Mossakowski.

6. Basque Culinary Center

Established in 2011, the Basque Culinary Center was created by the Mondragon University and a group of prominent Basque chefs becoming the first to officially offer culinary training in Spain. Split into two segments, it doesn't just train the chefs of tomorrow through the Faculty of Gastronomic Sciences, but also conducts research in the field of gastronomy through its Research and Innovation Center.

They offer everything, from bachelor's to master's to Ph.Ds in the Gastronomic Sciences, making it the perfect place for the scholars among you to immerse yourself in the science of food.

Institutes in the Middle East and India
1. The Oberoi Centre of Learning and Development (OCLD)

My alma mater, Oberoi Centre Learning Development programs in India are ranked amongst the best in Asia. And unlike many others, these are intensive programs where you live and breathe the hospitality industry. The best part? They don't just take care of accommodation, food, and even transport, you will also get a monthly allowance during your training period. But this also means they only take the cream of the crop and most days are spent immersed in real-world hospitality environments.

The first step, funnily enough, is STEP, the Systematic Training and Education Program. Their 36-month undergraduate program, this is perfect for those taking their first steps towards a formal culinary education. This program gives you a comprehensive view of not just the various kitchens, but also every other department that exists in a hotel providing you with an in-depth understanding of the hospitality industry.

The next step is OCLD, their graduate program, where you work towards your specialization in this case, Kitchen Management. This is an 18-24-month program that provides comprehensive classroom education as well as hands-on experience at award-winning Oberoi and Trident Hotels.

2. Taj Hotelier Development Program

The Taj group of hotels is world-renowned for their immaculate and exceptional experiences that transcend what any other chain offers. And in association with Tata Institute of Social Sciences, they offer a 3-year Bachelor of Vocation Degree in Hotel Management.

This program combines both classroom learning as well as on-the-job training, putting students right in the thick of things so that they learn from experience as much as they do from books. You can enroll at different Indian cities, with the program being offered at Taj Hotels in Mumbai, Delhi, NCR, Bengaluru, Kolkata, and Goa.

3. Institute of Hotel Management (IHM), Aurangabad

A joint initiative by the Taj group of hotels and the Maulana Azad Educational Trust, IHM Aurangabad was established in 1989.

Today, the institution offers two international degrees in Hotel Management and Culinary Arts, as well as a range of courses for personality and skill development to prepare students for a life in the hospitality industry.

4. International Culinary Centre for Arts (ICCA)

Located in Dubai, UAE, the International Culinary Centre for Arts was established in 2005 as the first school of its kind in the Middle East. Offering world-class culinary education, more than 80% of the hospitality businesses in the UAE are serviced by an ICCA graduate (their numbers, not mine!). Now that's astounding, right?

For those looking to get into a professional kitchen, they offer Professional Diploma Programs in both Cookery as well as Patisserie.

5. Emirates Academy of Hospitality Management (EAHM)

Located in an iconic area in Dubai, UAE, located just across the street from the luxurious Burj Al Arab, EAHM specializes in business management degrees with a focus on hospitality. Their internationally recognized programs, world-renowned faculty, modern facilities, and proximity to some of the best hotels in the world make it one of the go-to hospitality institutes.

They offer both undergraduate and postgraduate programs in hospitality, as well as several short training courses.

These are just a few of the options I looked at before I settled on Oberoi Centre for Learning and Development. But as I said, there is no right or wrong option here.

Find what works best for you. And jump right in.

I know, I know. That's easier said than done. And I'm sure a lot of you are still trying to picture where you would fit in in a professional kitchen.

To make it a little easier for you to see where you could do your best job, I'll take you through all the different stations in a professional kitchen that need to work together for the perfect service.

Stations in a Professional Kitchen

[Insert graphic to show the layout in a visual with each section highlighted]

1. Saucier Station

In many cuisines, the sauce in the star, the main attraction. At the Saucier Station is where the magic happens. The saucier is responsible for making sauces, as well as preparing all pan fried and sauteed food.

This is one of the most important stations in a professional kitchen, and it needs an experienced chef who is adept at managing complicated tasks and working with strict time constraints.

What you'll be cooking: Sauces, stews, gravies, and sauteed items.

2. Poissonnier Station

This station is where all the fish and seafood dishes are prepared. And if those dishes need accompanying sauces, they may also be prepared at this station rather than the Saucier Station.

The chefs working at this station may also have the responsibility of sourcing fresh fish and other seafood for dishes each day.

What you'll be cooking: Fish and seafood dishes, and accompanying sauces.

3. Rotisseur Station

If you've got a good eye for meat, then this will be the station for you. All the meat, both red and white, is prepared at this station in a variety of methods, depending on the cuisine being served.

Chefs working at this station may also be required to butcher their own meat. This means getting an understanding of how different cuts of meat bring out different flavors is quite important.

What you'll be cooking: Different cuts of meats and marinades.

4. Entremetier Station

Moving on to the vegetables (can't forget them). At the Entremetier Station, all the vegetables are prepared for the various dishes. In many restaurants, this station is also where soups are prepared.

Chefs working at this station need great knife skills and an understanding of how to balance subtle flavors.

What you'll be cooking: Soups, stocks and vegetable-based dishes.

5. Patissier Station

The course that makes or breaks a meal dessert. The Patissier Station is responsible for everything sweet. And in some restaurants, they also run the bakery, making bread, and other baked goods to be served to diners.

Chefs working at this station need a great understanding of chemistry and a deft hand. Because pastry work is an intricate art that needs a lot of skill.

What you'll be cooking: Desserts and baked goods.

See, there are a lot of different places for many different types of chefs to fit in in a professional kitchen. And no matter what your interests, I'm sure you'll find your own place there too.

And the first step towards that is to do your research. While I've given you a general idea of what you can expect, I'm sure there are certain parts that interest you. If you want to dive deeper into what goes on in a kitchen and how you can get started on your own journey, here are some great books that I found when I was doing my own research.

Some of them will guide you further on the path to a professional kitchen, some of them are memoirs of chefs that I've grown to admire deeply, and some are just books that I found inspiring as I started my own journey to become a chef.

1. The Flavor Bible by Andrew Dornenburg & Karen Page

If you're looking for the one book that will teach you everything there is to know about flavor, then this is it. The definitive guide to flavor, this book gives you great insight into classic ingredients, their origins and compositions, as well as the best pairings to go along with them.

An in-depth resource, you will want this by your side when you're experimenting with ingredients in the kitchen.

2. On Food and Cooking by Harold McGee

Written in 1984 by one of America's premier writers on cooking and culinary history, the contents of this book are still relevant all these years later. It offers great insight behind the science of cooking, such as how ingredients interact with each other and the importance of temperature.

You will be relieved to know that "scientific" doesn't mean "difficult to understand". The book is quite accessible to all types of readers, and is a useful addition to any would-be chef's library.

3. The Tummy Trilogy by Calvin Trillin

Okay, so this is actually a collection of Calvin Trillin's three most successful books American Fried; Alice, Let's Eat; and. Third Helpings This excellent chef's resource exudes passion for the simple things, and as you journey through 40 years of culinary knowledge crammed into one book, you'll start feeling that passion too.

Each chapter is simple, yet engaging, making it not just an informative read, but an enjoyable one too.

4. Great Chefs of France by Anthony Blake and Quentin Crewe

French cuisine has always held a magic and allure for most chefs, many thinking of it as the holy grail of cooking.

While I may not go that far, France has admittedly had an incomparable impact on the landscape of the culinary world.

Each of these five books follows a different three-starred-Michelin chef over the course of a typical day, while the chefs share their philosophy for food and talk about their inspirations. A great way to get insight into the thought process of some of the most influential chefs in modern history, this is the book for you if you want a better understanding of the industry.

5. The Devil in the Kitchen by Marco Pierre White

The youngest and the first chef to win three Michelin stars, perfection and Marco Pierre White go hand in hand. This book covers his entire culinary career, with its ups and downs, giving you great insight into the life of a chef that many look up to.

What I loved about this book are the many stories he shares about other famous chefs, many of whom trained under him, of course. It also gave me a deeper understanding of the devotion and dedication it takes to become a professional chef and it's something that's never left me after I put this book down.

6. Kitchen Confidential by Anthony Bourdain

Needless to say, Anthony Bourdain changed the face of travel and culinary shows on television with his hilarious, yet deep and insightful commentary on the food and lives of people of the countries he visited. This impact on the world's culinary landscape wasn't limited to television though.

In *Kitchen Confidential*, Anthony Bourdain shares true stories from his life as a professional chef for more than 25 years, all of them uncensored and all of them incredibly funny and wild. This memoir is a great read for every aspiring chef, if only for the insight into the interesting and weird world of Anthony Bourdain.

7. Mastering the Art of French Cooking by Julia Childs

Taking a slight detour from memoirs, this is the one-stop-shop for all the classic foods of France. Julia Childs, and contributors Simone Beck and Louisette Bertholle, arrange recipes in a sequence of themes and variations, with a focus on key recipes that form the backbone of French cooking.

If French cooking is your calling, then this book is a must-read, with over100 illustrations that make it easier to follow the steps and get a stronger understanding of the skills needed in French cooking.

8. Made in Italy by Giorgio Locatelli

Giorgio Locatelli is one of the greatest Italian chefs of all time. And this book, with its 624 vibrantly illustrated pages full of his recipes, insight and historical detail about Italian food, is one of the greatest books about Italian food. The book is full of evocative and funny stories, with witty observations on the food culture of today.

Filled to the brim with passion and gastronomic brilliance, if Italian cuisine is your calling, then this book written by the master of modern Italian cooking should be your food bible.

9. Cooking Delights of the Maharajas by Digvijaya Singh

The Maharajas, or kings, of India were known for their penchant for opulence and luxury. And this extended to their choice of food as well. This book catalogs the most opulent recipes of that time, with a collection of exotic dishes and styles that bring the past to life.

I love taking inspiration from the past and creating a modern twist to it, and I find myself going back and flipping through the pages of this book once in a while, just taking in the grand scale in which things were done back in the days of the Maharajas.

10. The Making of a Chef by Michael Ruhlman

Even if you don't end up studying at the Culinary Institute of America, this book gives you a great look at life there as you follow Michaels Ruhlman's journey towards mastering the art of cooking during his time at the institute.

It is a great read for would-be culinary students as you get to see in vivid detail what life is when you're training to be a chef. And it's no walk in the park.

These are just some of the many books I devoured as I did my research, and I hope these will help you too. These, and many other books by amazing chefs and authors, are a great way to expand your knowledge and get inspired to blaze your own trail.

I keep picking up books like these even now, because learning never ends. And reading about other chef's experiences, or recipes, inspires me to keep innovating and trying new things.

After all, as a chef, especially today, you really can't stand still.

Chapter 4: Gaining Experience

Now that you have a clearer idea of the possible paths to a professional kitchen, I think it is the perfect time to introduce you all to a concept of which some of you may not be familiar—staging.

So, what is staging?

Originating from the French word, stagiaire, staging is essentially an internship where a budding chef such as you (or even ones with experience) works in another chef's kitchen for a brief period of time. This not only gives you the opportunity to learn from some of the best chefs in the business but also allows you to pick up new skills and techniques, as well as deeper insight into a particular cuisine that you may not get from formal culinary education. However, it is definitely an unpaid position, and that is something you should keep in mind.

When I finished my OCLD, I wasn't really sure where I wanted to work next, or even what cuisine I wanted to specialize in. All I knew was that I wanted to learn and grow as much as possible.

But how?

And then it dawned on me that I should apply to work as a stage in some of the best restaurants in the world. Simple.

As you may expect, it turned out to not be simple at all, especially because at that time, it was almost unheard of for a young Indian chef to go abroad and stage in some of the best restaurants in the world. Which also meant that I did not have much of a guide to follow; everything had to be researched and planned on my own.

The process began a year before I even stepped foot into one of these restaurants, starting with writing my stagiaire letter, and let me tell you that this was harder than any experience I've had in a kitchen. I constantly wrote and rewrote sections. I showed the letter to multiple people to get their opinions. I kept second-guessing how it would be perceived. Basically, I twisted myself inside out to make sure it was perfect.

Now was it perfect? I don't really know. All I know is that it opened a few doors for me. And to help you get a good start to writing to your own, I've included a copy of my stagiaire letter below:

My name is Nigel Lobo. I grew up in Dubai, UAE, moved to Bangalore, India in 2008 and went for an on-the-job training program called STEP (Systematic Training and Education Program) at The Oberoi, Bangalore working in different sections in the kitchen over a period of three years.

Upon graduating last year, I started with my Post Graduate Diploma in Kitchen Management at the Oberoi Centre of Learning and Development, I will finish in July next year. My first exposure as an associate was The Oberoi Amarvilas in Agra and I'm currently doing my professional experience at the Trident Hotel in Gurgaon.

Currently I plan to stage after the completion of my course at your esteemed restaurant and I will commence traveling early July next year. Afterwards I hope to stay in the USA for another couple months interning somewhere currently undetermined, or return to India to work in an also undetermined restaurant.

At this point I have an amazing amount of opportunities, but nothing specifically set. The next couple of weeks will determine which direction my life will head at least for the foreseeable time. Which I think is pretty exciting.

For most Indian people circumstances govern their choice of profession, for me it's been my palette.

I really love good food and always wanted to become a really good chef. An artist's creation feeds the sight, a musician's work appeals to our ears – however food is that medium of creation that transcends many senses. I am sure you will agree.

I am passionate about everything I do, especially food and every time I get an opportunity I sneak into the kitchen and cook up a storm.

I am also always looking for the next best bite. I've devoted my life to eating well, cooking with others and sharing stories, usually centered around food.

I am absolutely clear that I want to start of a stage at your restaurant and is of high importance, and I can say this without any doubt that I will be highly honored if considered worthy of admission and will do everything within my reach to perform to expectations if not exceed them.

My experience till now has given me 'some food for thought' and fueled my curiosity and passion for a career in cooking and has enabled me to be a service-oriented team player thereby building strong working relationships and being flexible to changing priorities. My ability to set priorities, use initiative and work in a dynamic environment have made me a Capable Leader who has strong attention to detail, excellent interpersonal, written communication and negotiation skills.

It is with this drive to win and excel I am applying to stage at your esteemed restaurant. I believe studying at a restaurant in the USA would mean the best of both worlds for me. I would be studying at a world class restaurant of international repute with top notch professional chefs as well as in a cosmopolitan city like the USA – a melting point of varied cultures and cuisines.

My goal is only to get valuable experience from working in your restaurant and learn and absorb as much as I can from there which will help me in my career as a chef. My dream is to work for a Michelin starred restaurant, hopefully yours. I believe being selected at your restaurant will cement my future as a successful, creative and forward-thinking chef.

The next step was to figure out where to apply. And this is the most important thing to consider when you're planning your stagiaire applying to the right restaurants. When deciding restaurants to which you want to apply, there are quite a few factors that could drive your decision. You may want to learn from a particular chef. Or maybe you've been curious about a particular type of cuisine. Or maybe you just love the ethos and history of a particular restaurant. Whatever the reason, just make sure you have one. Because staging for the sake of staging is not going to help you in the way you really want to grow as a chef.

For me, it was about working with some of the most creative chefs in the world; who were doing things no one else was doing; exploring ingredients others ignored; redefining their cuisines in ways that were unimaginable just a few years ago.

And for this, I put together a list of the best restaurants in the world, turning to the San Pellegrino 50 Best Restaurants in the World, as well as a lot of other Michelin star restaurants I admired that didn't make the cut. And with my stagiaire letter and this list in hand, I began my quest for the opportunity to work at some of the leading and genre-defining restaurants in the world.

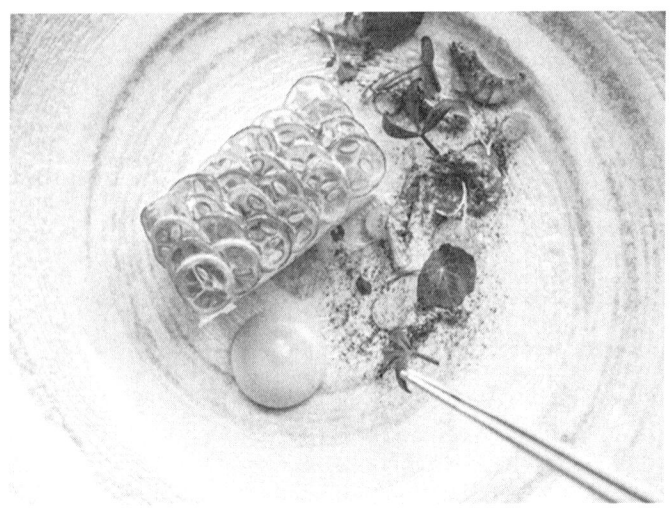

Lucky for me, in today's world, you don't have to try too hard to find a way to contact these restaurants. I just went to their websites, found their email addresses and sent them the pre-formatted letter to which I made a few minor changes depending on the restaurant and the impression I wanted to make.

With the easy part done, now all I could do was wait.

And wait I did. For quite a while.

I didn't hear back from anyone for six months. I would spend entire days with my eyes glued to my email inbox, constantly refreshing it to see if I finally got a reply. As you can guess, not a great way to spend your time both in terms of productivity and for your peace of mind.

But I didn't give up. I kept sending out letters one after the other. The inner fire that kept my hopes up, that kept me going, was still burning strong.

Then the first letter popped up in my inbox. Was it an opportunity to live my dream?

No, it wasn't.

Instead, it was a very politely-worded letter telling me they were full at the moment, but I should definitely apply in a year's time. And you know what? After waiting for so long for a reply, even a rejection felt like an achievement. A very minor one, but an achievement nonetheless.

After all, this meant that someone was reading my email. There was still hope.

Then I received another rejection letter, as polite as the previous one, but basically saying the same thing. Then another; and another; and another.

By the fifth one, the roaring fire in my belly that I mentioned had simmered to what could be best described as a dwindling flame.

And then, after almost a year of applying to various restaurants came two emails one after the other that completely changed my life.

One was from La Vie in Osnabrück, Germany holders of three Michelin Stars. And the other was from Attica in Melbourne, Australia, the 23rd best restaurant in the world at that time.

As you can imagine, I couldn't hide my excitement, running around my house hugging my mom, shouting at the top of my lungs. All the embarrassing things one does when they've almost given up hope and then they finally see a ray of opportunity. Yes, the position they were offering was that of a Junior Sous Chef. But I didn't care. All I wanted to do was learn, whatever the designation they offered.

Now, you may be forgiven if you assumed that after this all I had to do was pack my bags and fly out to the restaurant of my choice. In fact, this was just the beginning of a long and winding process that included filling out forms, providing the restaurant with the required documentation, and most importantly, arranging for the visa.

And remember how I mentioned that this was an unpaid position? That also means the restaurant doesn't pay you to fly down to them. You take care of your tickets, your accommodation, your spending money. All of it.

As someone who was only 22 at that time, I barely had enough to take care of my own expenses let alone fund trips to both Germany and Australia. But I was lucky enough to have parents who believed in me and my passion, supporting me through these times. To be honest, they didn't really know or understand the culinary world or the importance of gaining experience working at these restaurants. They didn't even know what a "stage" was. They only asked me if it would help my career and that was it. Documentation and visa procedures were done and I was finally off to live my dream.

First, I landed in Germany, and as soon as I entered the kitchen at La Vie, I realized how little I actually knew about working in a professional kitchen. Even fileting a fish, you could see the attention and focus each chef put on the filet, ensuring every slice, every cut was perfect so the filet could be perfect. Here, I learned how to work for 14-15 hours tirelessly, but still striving for perfection with everything that leaves your section. But it was also not all work. In the month and a half I spent there, I made great friends and got the opportunity to see more of Germany, taking in their culture and cuisine.

It was here where I heard about a course offered in Spain, where they choose only one young chef from each country to come live and work in Spain for six months, learning about the local culture, history, and cuisine. And while I did not jump at it right then and there, this was one opportunity that was always in the back of my head.

After I came back to Dubai from Germany, the next destination was Australia. Attica was the best restaurant in Australia at that moment, and once I started working in the kitchen, I knew exactly why. Each day, only the freshest produce would come into the kitchen, all local, all grown or sourced from nearby. And most importantly, there was a focus on using the entire ingredient and minimizing wastage.

So we would start our day by taking a trip to the restaurant farm which was just 5 minutes away from where we would get some of the ingredients we needed for the day. If we had 50 guests coming in and each plate needed a frond of herbs, then we would pluck exactly 51 fronds. That was the extent to which the restaurant and everyone working there was dedicated to minimizing waste.

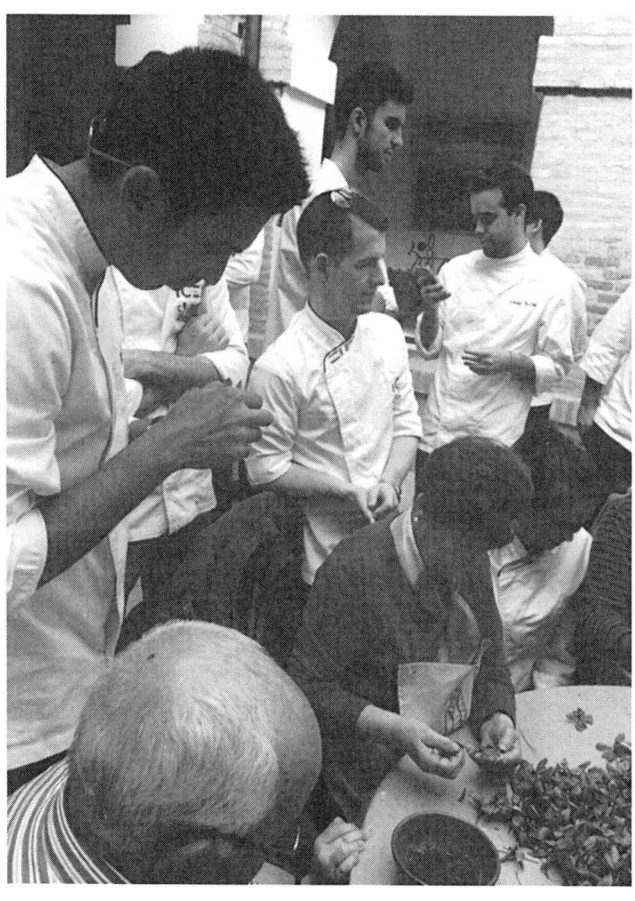

The cuisine and culture were poles apart from each other at both places, giving me a great perspective on how food, and the overall culinary culture, is viewed and experienced in different parts of the world.

My experiences in Germany and Australia had helped me add a lot of new skills and techniques to my repertoire. But I still wanted more. However, by now, it was time for me to go back to The Oberoi and take up my posting that was waiting for me at The Oberoi Udaivillas. After all, I had promised them that I would come back and join them after my staging experiences. But in the back of my mind, the Spanish course and the possibilities it would open up still kept playing over and over.

So I applied for it with no hope that I would get selected, to be honest; but then, I was selected. Which meant it was time for me to approach my boss at The Oberoi once again and tell them that I had to leave. While my immediate head was supportive, the rest of the higher ups didn't take too kindly to me leaving again so soon after I had come back. But my mind was set. I wanted to learn and grow, and that would only happen if I left The Oberoi, got out of my comfort zone and jumped at this opportunity. And it was only once I reached Spain that I truly saw the scope of this opportunity, and how lucky I was to be a part of it.

The course itself had 13 chefs from 13 different countries and was split into two parts, some months learning about Spain, the language, the culture, the food, and the rest working at a Michelin starred restaurant in an area of Spain.

For the first few months, mornings would be filled with Spanish lessons and learning about Spanish history and culture. Then we would all go work in tapas restaurants in the area until dinner. Hectic, yes. But also one of the most fun experiences I've had. Once this initial period was over, came the exciting moment all of us would be assigned to a Michelin starred restaurant in which we would work. And all of them were assigned a restaurant; me, I was assigned two. I didn't bother asking how or why. I just jumped at the opportunity, watching and learning every moment I spent at both these places.

Apart from this, I also got the opportunity to explore different parts of the world and make new friends. And it was these friends that kept me calm and sane when I was stressed out and homesick. The bonds I formed during my time as a stage are still strong and I make sure to keep in touch with all the great people I met during my time in Germany, Australia, and Spain.

Now, obviously, I'm sure you're excited to start emailing restaurants to start your own stage experience. But life is not all rosy and full of happy new experiences when you're a stagier. Because when you're a stagier, you essentially start from the bottom again. Every time. Cutting; portioning; cleaning. You'll do all of that and a lot more of the basics when you start off your stage experience. But if you're ready to take a chance on yourself and really want to learn, there is no better way to grow as a chef.

It's my experiences as a stagier that really made me stand out from the rest when I was ready to head out on my own. It taught me how different kitchens work; what it means to cook the right way; how I could use ingredients in combinations I could not even begin to imagine. And most importantly, it gave me an insider's view into the world of Michelin kitchens at an age where most people had only seen them, and Michelin star chefs, on TV. The lessons I learned from there about perfection are something I carry with me even today.

In fact, I would go as far as to say that I truly started on the journey to becoming the chef I am today only after my experiences in Osnabruck and Melbourne.

So how can you make sure you get the most out of your stage experience? Well, I have a few tips that can help you get started on the right foot.

1. If you don't know Ask

   As a stagier, no one expects you to know everything. That's why it is important to always ask questions, even if you think it may annoy the person who you're pestering. After all, it is better than pretending you know how to make a coq au vin when you have no idea what any of those words mean.

2. Carry something to write on

   During your stage experience, you will be constantly bombarded with new information. New recipes, new ingredients, new cooking techniques. But if you don't have a notepad where you can take everything down, you're going to be left with smudges on your arm that you'll struggle to decipher once you get back to your room.

3. Choose where you stage

This is something I mentioned earlier, but it is so important that I would be remiss if I didn't include it here. Staging is a very personal experience, and what works for one budding chef may not work for another. Set yourself very clear goals on what you want to achieve from your staging experience, and then choose where you would like to work accordingly.

4. Stay strong

Staging, especially in a foreign country where you barely know anyone, can be a very stressful experience. And when you add to that working with a three Michelin starred chef and trying to live up to those "Michelin star" expectations, it is natural that sooner rather than later you will be overwhelmed and overawed. Most nights will be long; many of them will be difficult. But trust me when I say you will emerge a better chef after the experience.

5. Find a good vantage point

Sometimes you may find yourself on the sidelines while the rest of the kitchen is in full flow and all that will be expected of you is to observe and learn. This is when you need to find the perfect vantage point from where you can see everyone in action, and with your notepad in hand, take in the controlled chaos that is a world-class kitchen in full swing.

6. Socialize

   No matter at which restaurant you end up staging, the time you have there will be limited. So make sure you pick the brains of as many people as possible, from the juniors to the senior-most, because they'll all have something to teach you.

These are just a few things that I learned from my times as a stage; things that I hope will help you on your journey to becoming a successful chef yourself. But if there is one thing that I hope you take from my experiences, it is that you shouldn't give up. Keep at it, and sooner or later, the right opportunity will show itself.

Chapter 5:
The Importance of a Mentor

I'm sure you'll agree with me when I say that as an aspiring chef, there is a lot you don't know. And what you do know may be limited to your own personal experiences and opportunities for learning. In such a scenario, how does a budding chef find direction and the opportunity to be the best chef they can be?

By finding the right mentor, of course!

While the benefits of mentorship are quite evident and self-explanatory in many industries, its role and impact in the culinary world is second to none. Ask any successful chef and they'll tell you that they wouldn't have reached the heights they have if they didn't have the mentors they did.

In fact, I don't think I'd be where I am today if it wasn't for the mentors, I had the opportunity to meet along the way. And it's not just in the time and effort they put in helping you learn. It is also the faith they show in you, pushing you forward, that makes all the difference.

When I started off in Bangalore, India as a STEP trainee I had chefs in every section who took time out to teach me. Take making something as simple as pizza as an example. They could have just taught me how it's done and that should have been enough. Instead, they taught me about its history; the different types of dough; the tradition and cultural significance of pizzas; why different tomatoes are used. And it is these small things that really add up and mold you into the chef you will become.

After STEP came OCLD, the management training program where it was more about theory than the practical aspects of running a kitchen. And even there, the chefs with whom I ended up meeting and interacting for whatever short period of time, really left an impact on me in terms of their work ethic and the investment they made in helping me learn and grow.

It is during one of these training sessions that I met my first true mentors Chef Vikas Vichare. One of the first experiences I remember sharing with him is putting together a 15-course tasting menu. This was something completely new to me and I remember sweating through my chef whites with nervousness. But he was there through it all and helped me really understand the nitty gritty of what was needed. And needless to say, by the end of service, we had formed great camaraderie that exists till today.

My stages also played a huge role in my growth allowing me to create relationships that I could leverage later in my career when I started off on my own. And it's not just the Michelin star chefs I learned from. Because a lot of my interactions were with the head chefs at both La Vie and Attica, I ended up learning much more from them than I could ever imagine.

And no conversation about my mentors is complete without Chef Jitin Joshi, who worked as the head chef at Banaras, run by Chef Atul Kochhar, when they won their first Michelin star in 2001. I had the opportunity to meet him when I landed back in Dubai after my stage experiences in Germany and Australia in 2015. When I met him for the first time, he was working for a different group. But when he moved to the Taj Group, he offered me the chance of a lifetime, to work as Chef de Cuisine at the Eloquent Elephant, a new gastropub that the Taj Group was just starting.

To put this in context, I was just 24. While my resume looked impressive this is where my stage experience really helped. I didn't really think I was more skilled or talented than anyone else my age in the industry. In fact, even now, I don't think I would be able to put that much trust and faith in a 24-year-old with such an important role and all the responsibilities it comes with, no matter how impressive his resume was.

But he saw something different.

It was a huge step for me running the kitchen at the Eloquent Elephant. And his trust paid off once we started winning awards for our food across the region. And I think it was after we won our first award for Best Pub Grub in the UAE that I actually asked him the question that I had wanted to ask right from when he offered me the position.

"Why me? What made you trust a relatively untested aspiring chef with such a huge responsibility?"

To this, he had a very simple answer.

He said, "I saw a fire in you. It wasn't about your resume, your experience or even the skills you had. It was the passion I saw radiating from you a passion to learn and grow. And that's what I trusted."

Inspiring stuff, isn't it? I definitely thought so, because that conversation stuck with me, and now it keeps pushing me forward to explore new avenues and break new ground.

He was, and still is one of the most influential people in my life. And if you asked me which lesson from him that I cherish most, I would tell you it has nothing to do with cuisine or cooking techniques; it's how he managed people that really inspired me.

You know there are certain questions to which the answer will always be "No". But I used to love asking him these questions, just to see how he would react and handle it. How artfully he would mold his response. And it's all these interactions that have influenced the way I interact and talk to the people who work with me especially when I'm in a tough situation. Because, in tough situations, you will look up to the people you admire, think about what they would do and then react based on what you've learned. And I think that's the most important part of having a mentor.

While you're learning and growing, they obviously show you the way. But once you reach a point where you're out there on your own, their point of view and values really guide the way you behave, teach, and work.

In fact, it is because of my mentor Chef Bali that I had the opportunity to put my first degustation menu together. That too for some very important guests, including Mr. Vishveshwar Raj Singh, GM, Trident Bandra Kurla, Mumbai, Executive Chef Rohit Gambhir and F&B Service Manager Anand Chatterjee. I was told to go all out, and let my creativity and passion for food shine through. And that's what I did. Putting together and executing a menu that I was truly proud of. Here's what the menu looked like.

APPETISER

Cannolo
goat cheese, tomato and olive

Tomato and mozzarella salad
three ways

Tenderloin tartare

pecorino ice, horseradish cream and sprouts
Cinnamon fried chicken
polenta and corn

SOUP

Ligurian minestrone

PASTA

butter, pepper and pecorino

Potato and leek ravioli
prosciutto crisp and parmesan air

SORBET
White wine granita

MAIN COURSE
Snapper with crisp scales
spiced wine must, carrots and zucchini
Balsamic and honey braised pork belly
house rub, green peas and morels

DESSERT
Fruits of Antarctica

Chocolate and milk
textures

Dear Mohit and Chef Bali,

This afternoon, Chef Nigel Lobo (Kitchen Management Associate – Executive Stage) invited four of us for lunch in Botticino, to sample a menu conceived and prepared by him. Not suspecting what we were in for, Executive Chef Rohit Gambhir, F&B Service Manager Anand Chatterjee, my wife Sanaya and I walked straight into his "sucker punch"!

Over the next 75 minutes, Nigel put out 12 exquisitely prepared dishes (the menu is attached) which impressed us all with the technical proficiency, creativity and eye for detail that they represented. Each item was sophisticated in its presentation, with subtle textures and well-balanced flavors that showcased Nigel's culinary skills brilliantly. Unfortunately, we were all so enamored by the food that we completely forgot to take photographs – save for one of the snappers, which is attached.

I think I speak for all of us when I say that we had one of the most memorable meals we've eaten in a long while!

However, the real highlight of the afternoon for me was discovering Nigel's mature-beyond-his-years talent and obvious passion for his work. He conceived this experience entirely on his own, and went above and beyond the parameters of his training schedule to make it happen. I am so proud and happy that Trident, Bandra Kurla and the kitchen team in Botticino could provide the appropriate environment for him to bring his culinary ideas to fruition.

I must applaud you individually, and OCLD as a whole, for nurturing Nigel's potential and enthusiasm over the past 1½ years.

If there is anything that the team at Trident, Bandra Kurla or I can do to facilitate his learning and development for continued success, please know that we'd be very happy to do so.

Needless to say, I was over the moon – and none of this would have been possible without my mentors.

I would even go as far as to say that you really don't understand or appreciate the true value of what you're learning. But when you look back at all these experiences later, you realize how deep of an impact the mentors have had on you, especially when you're in the position your mentors were in. Because it is only then you realize the stress and struggles that they were going through behind the scenes that you never saw because that's how good they were.

And then you get perspective.

When I sit and look back at my experiences now, I can honestly say that I was lucky to find people throughout my journey towards becoming a professional chef who put their trust in me; pushing me forward even when I doubted my own potential. And that's why I place such a huge importance on having the right mentor.

Now I'm sure you're wondering, how do I find a mentor?

Well, there is no real way to go out there and find a mentor. Instead a mentor finds you. All you can do is put yourself in the best position to attract someone who believes in you and your potential.

For that to happen, you need to understand a very simple, yet powerful point: no one will be as invested in your career growth and development as much as you will be.

Yes, a mentor will take an interest in you and teach you what they know, guiding you in the right direction. But in the end, your career is in your hands.

You need to show an interest in upgrading yourself; a willingness to take responsibilities that are a step above your paygrade. You need to prove yourself by going about and beyond what your job requirement requires. That is what will show your drive to learn, grow and be the best you can be, the more likely you are to attract a mentor who will be invested in you and your career.

Because mentors help those who help themselves. And you need to show them that you are worth the time and effort they will put into helping you grow.

To help you along the way, here are a few things that I learned through my experiences that can help you make the most of your mentor-mentee relationship.

First, look and ask around.

This is a tricky one, because your first instinct is to approach the one with the most impressive title. But in my experience, it is not the title but a willingness to teach that really matters. Start with the chef or sous chef; and if they don't have the time or inclination, ask them if they can direct you to someone who does.

Second, work on creating a beneficial mentor-mentee relationship.

When a mentor takes you under their wing, your only responsibility is to take in everything they teach you and see how you can incorporate it into your life, both inside and outside the kitchen. It is also important to remember that your relationship, at least at the start, is still going to be a professional one. Yes, it is possible that eventually the relationship will grow into something that is deeper, but you need to let that happen naturally and not jump the gun.

Third, there is no fixed lifecycle for a mentor-mentee relationship.

While there is no such thing as a fixed lifecycle for a mentor-mentee relationship, there are some that you will outgrow as you progress in your career. Now that doesn't mean the relationship ends. All that means is that they will not be looking over your shoulder day in and day out. What they teach you will guide you and your career for years to come.

Fourth, trust the process.

Like any other relationship, a mentor-mentee connection develops over time. The ones that are successful are not forced. They are forged from mutual admiration and shared experiences. So don't rush it.

Fifth, and the most important, put yourself out there.

As I mentioned earlier, you will find the right mentor only when you show the hunger and desire to learn and grow. So put yourself out there and show that you are willing to learn. And sooner rather than later, the right mentor will definitely come along.

Chapter 6:
Growing Your Brand

I'm sure you're wondering what this chapter is all about.

After all, as a chef, your brand is the food you cook and the culinary creativity you show, isn't it? And once you become an experienced chef, the next step is to open a restaurant of your own, right?

In a way yes; but also no.

Today, any chef worth his salt will tell you that growing their own brand is as important to career growth as is a flair for doing something different and creative. This is because in today's highly connected, always-on world, chefs have evolved from people who just prepare delicious food. Today, they are rock stars who are inspiring people world over to pick up their knives and spatulas and dive into the world of cooking up food from all over the world.

How many of these names have you heard Gordon Ramsey, Jamie Oliver, Tim Curtis and Gary Mehigan? Some, if not all them, right?

They all have restaurants across the world. But the true brand isn't the restaurant. It is them and their name. They are the ones who appear on various TV shows. They are the ones for whom people travel half-way across the world after having waited months and years for a single reservation. Today, chefs are a bigger brand than the restaurants.

And if you want to start your own and operate your own restaurant somewhere down the line, then it is important that you start focusing on establishing a brand to which people will flock and that is your name.

But how do you make sure your name gets out there for everyone to see?

That's exactly what I'm here to help you with.

The first thing to know is that when you enter the culinary world today, you are entering one of the most competitive industries there is. A mix of factors, including the spread of cooking reality TV shows and the growth of gastronomy, has made the culinary industry a much sought-after place to work. And just like you, there will be hundreds and thousands of chefs who will want to rise to the top and become known for their culinary skills and techniques.

Just a decade or two ago, if you were working for a high-profile restaurant in one of the major cities in the world, all you needed to make a name for yourself and get the recognition you deserve was to be an exceptional chef. But not anymore. While culinary knowledge and skill is still very important, it is also important to build your brand as a chef.

But what is this "personal brand" I keep talking about?

To break it down into simple terms, it is basically how the world sees you and your career. That's it. And what makes your personal brand is what sets you apart from the rest; what makes you unique and relevant as a chef. When faced with countless chefs doing the recipes, cooking videos, and blog posts online, it is the chef with a distinct brand personality that will stand out.

Does that sound hard? Once you figure out what really sets you apart, you'll realize that it really isn't. And the first step is to see what some of the chefs you love and follow are doing to grow their brand and attract an audience. Here are some of the things I learned from my favorite chefs when I got down to the process of branding myself.

And to help you along the way, here are a few tips and tricks I have learned in the process of branding myself.

1. *Produce content that people value*

    The best way to create a loyal following is to create and put out content that will add value to people's lives; something they will connect with and appreciate. This will put you out there as a brand, showcasing you, your talents and your ideas to the world. At the same time, it is important to engage your audience—which is where social media becomes a great tool to stay connected and offer value to your audience. And as your following grows, you will get a better idea of what is working and what is, allowing you to further boost your popularity and spread your brand.

2. *Share content that people will love*

    I know better than most how stressful life is when you're just starting off a career as a chef. This means creating regular content and sharing it with your audience is next to impossible. But what you can do is curate content that your audience will find valuable and interesting, which not only gives them an idea of what you like, but also provides them with something to look forward to—even if you're not creating original content.

3. *Use the right tools*

Today, there are a plethora of platforms one can use to get conversations started and grow a brand. From social media platforms such as Facebook and Twitter to content platforms such as YouTube and Medium—all of them allow you to target and find the right audience for your content, connecting you to a section of the population that you know is interested and finds value in what you have to offer. These tools require absolutely no investment and are so readily available to connect with like-minded individuals that finding people who will love your content becomes so much easier than it used to be. And I can't emphasize enough on the importance of the groundwork this lays to create a strong and long-lasting relationship with your audience.

4. *Get noticed*

While online tools have made connecting with people all over the world easier than ever, sometimes there is no replacement for good old fashioned face-to-face connections. And making these connections is incredibly easy once you know where to look for them. From industry events and meet-ups to something as simple as a food festival, connections are waiting to be made at every step—all you need to do is to put yourself out there and be willing to show the authentic you to the people around. Another way to grow your brand is to create relationships that are based on good faith by becoming a part of charitable events or offering to help smaller brands in whatever way you can. This creates a foundation that you can leverage at a later time when you require it.

5. *Be you*

Throughout this chapter, we have been talking about your brand as if it is something distinct from you. But that should never be the case. While there are brands that have been created with a particular image and tone in mind to attract a very specific audience, if you want to succeed in building and growing yourself as a brand, you need to be the most authentic version of yourself as possible in every interaction you have. This is because what you're looking to create isn't a following of people who like you for what you post. Instead, your aim should be to create a following who are like-minded and resonate with everything you do. When you're successful in doing this, that's when you'll have a brand that will transcend pure "likes" and "shares" and truly become a part of your audience's life.

Now obviously, what may have worked for me may not work for you. Or by the time you're reading this, Facebook has already gone the way of Myspace and Orkut, and now there is a new social media giant in town. What I'm trying to say is that with changing times, the way you do things transforming yourself into a brand in this case will also evolve and change. But what should remain the same is your authenticity and a desire to put your content out to the world to make a difference, any difference, in the way people think or live.

If your uniqueness succeeds in making even tiny inroads into your desired audience's mind, then rest assured that sooner or later, your brand will be able to spread its wings and fly high on the currents of success and recognition.

But that doesn't mean you sacrifice growing as a chef; because first, and foremost, that's what you are. So spend a majority of your time honing your culinary knowledge, skills and technique, and see how you can mold and adapt your learnings into meaningful and interesting content for your future audience.

The best part? You can start right away. Even this very moment.

Chapter 7:
Starting Your Own Restaurant

Now you've done everything you needed to.

You've spent time traveling, staging under great chefs and learning all there is to learn about different ingredients, cuisines and cooking techniques.

You've built your brand to such a level that you have a loyal audience who loves and admires you and is genuinely interested in what you do and have to say.

You've worked at different restaurants and hotels, honing your skills, climbing up the ladder and taking on more responsibility.

After all this, you finally have a great understanding of your own personal food dream, the ingredients you want to champion, the techniques you want to showcase, and the cuisine you want to explore.

But you've reached a point where you feel that as long as you work at someone else's restaurant, your creativity and sense of personal expression is stifled. You want to let loose and truly let your culinary voice be heard.

And you see that the only path that takes you towards realizing your culinary dream is to open a restaurant of your own. Maybe not the 100-seater that you've been used to serving every day. But something that you can call your own.

That's great. But before you go and drop in your resignation, maybe you should have a plan in place, right? So how do you go about starting your own restaurant?

Well I'm glad you asked, because trust me, it is not as easy as you think. It involves juggling a lot of moving parts that need to be constantly managed. And you need to be more than just a great chef to run a restaurant that is successful.

To help you understand everything that goes into starting your own restaurant, I've broken down a few aspects that you need to consider before you even think about serving your first customer.

Who Will You Serve?

When it comes to food, everyone has a preference. That is obvious. As much as you want to create a place that everyone, and by that I mean everyone, will love to visit and experience, it is not realistically possible. And if you do try to attract everyone, you'll most probably end up attracting no one at all. This means you need to have a clear idea of the audience you are targeting right from the start, even if that is only 10-15% of the market, and focus on them.

So what are the main target markets for a food-service business? Let us have a look.

1. The Millennials

> A term used for anyone born between 1980 and 2000, millennials are most likely to be open to trying new things and new places.

2. Generation X

A term used for anyone born between 1965 and 1980, this demographic is family-oriented and is most likely to be attracted by a comfortable atmosphere and value for money.

3. Baby Boomers

A term used for anyone born between 1946 and 1964, most of the people in this demographic are grandparents, which means they tend to prefer restaurants that offer a family-friendly atmosphere. Many of the baby boomers also have children who have left the family home and now live away from them. This section of baby boomers are less concerned about price and more concerned about the experience the restaurant provides.

4. Seniors

A term used for people who are above the age of 65, Seniors are generally on a fixed income. This means their choice of restaurants will be those that offer good service at reasonable prices.

Does that give you a better idea of who you want to target your restaurant towards?

No? Maybe these questions will help you finetune the demographic you want to attract.

1. *Who are they?*

    Are they old or young? Married or unmarried? Do they have children?

2. *What do they do?*

    What sort of job do they do? How much do they earn? What's their income bracket?

3. *What do they like to eat?*

    Do they experiment with different cuisines? Are they open to trying exotic ingredients?

4. *When do they visit?*

    Do they like coming in for a quick lunch? Do they come in only for dinner? Do they prefer a lazy brunch?

5. *How long do they stay?*

    Do they come in only to have a quick bite? Do they like taking their time? Do they treat it like a social occasion and spend the entire evening hanging out in a group?

When you sit down and think of your hypothetical customer and try to answer these questions about them, you are sure to get a clearer idea of the demographic you want to attract. And then you can plan the rest accordingly.

What service style will you offer?

If you look at most of the restaurants around you, you can generally break them down into three different categories: quick-service, midscale, and upscale. Figuring out where you want to position is very important as it will give you a clearer idea of the type of food you will offer, size of restaurant you will need, and even the margins you will earn once you get started.

I've broken down each of these styles below so you can get a clearer idea of what they represent, so you can best choose where your restaurant idea will fit in.

Quick-Service Restaurant

Quick-service or fast-food restaurants generally offer a limited menu at a relatively low price, making them accessible to a much larger audience. Additionally, the seating arrangement is quite casual, and may also include a drive-through or take-away option. These restaurants serve a wide range of food, the defining characteristics of which are things that are quick to prepare, easy to eat, and easy on the wallet.

Midscale Restaurants

Midscale restaurants sit between fast food and upscale restaurants. This means they offer a wider range of options to customers as compared to a fast-food restaurant, but are priced at a price point that customer would generally think of as offering good value. Midscale restaurants have to focus more on the seating arrangements as well as on the ambience, offering customers an environment where they can sit and enjoy their meals.

Upscale Restaurants

Upscale restaurants are all about the experience. Customers who visit such restaurants generally don't think of the price; their primary aim is to enjoy great food in a great ambience. These restaurants are at the higher end of dining and can charge the highest prices, but also face the most scrutiny. This means you need to give utmost attention to every single detail right from the decor and lighting to the ingredients and even the plates on which the food is served.

While these three are the broad categories, there are many different sub-categories that each of these restaurant styles can be broken down into. But if you focus on figuring out where your future restaurant fits when it comes to these categories, you'll be well on your way.

What is Your Food Concept?

If you're like me, then you've been thinking about your food dream from the moment you set foot into a professional kitchen. If nothing, maybe you have an idea of the cuisine you want to serve at your restaurant, right? But it doesn't end there.

In today's highly competitive culinary world, you need to set your restaurant apart in every way possible to attract, and keep, a steady flow of clientele. And one of the most important facets of a restaurant that will help you stand out is by having a food concept that sets you apart from the rest;

something that really brings your idea and dream to life; something that communicates your food journey and story.

Does that sound like a tough ask? To help you on the way, I've listed down a few popular restaurant concepts that you can use as the base to create your own unique twist to what people know and love.

1. Ethnic Restaurants

As the world gets smaller and smaller, you will see a lot more ethnic restaurants across every major city in the world. Showcasing cuisine from a different part of the world, and using ingredients that are mostly used only in that cuisine, these restaurants are the flag bearers spreading their cuisine to the rest of the world.

However, as popular as these restaurants have become, serving authentic ethnic cuisine is a must if you want to make sure that your restaurant becomes the must-visit place to experience the said cuisine.

2. Coffee Shop

Who doesn't love coffee, right? And if you don't believe that coffee has taken over the world, all you need to do is look out your window and you'll see at least one coffee shop down your street. But coffee shops are more than just a place to grab a cup of your favorite brew. It has also become a hub where people meet friends, a place to work while staying energized, or even just a place to spend some time before you head out to do whatever you have planned.

This means a coffee shop has become more than just coffee. That's why most serve an assortment of baked goods, desserts and even their own special coffee that they roast and ground to specifications.

3. Bakery

With more and more people realizing the benefits both in terms of health and in terms of taste of freshly made goods, bakeries have become increasingly popular, and have evolved from a place that only used to sell hot and fresh bread. Today, they offer cakes, scones, drinks, and even full menus of food such as sandwiches and hot entrees.

Starting a bakery offers a lot of opportunities to grow your business and make a name for yourself. But be warned, this is a space with a huge amount of competition which means you'll need to offer something unique and truly spectacular to keep the customers coming in day in and day out.

4. Delicatessen

Delicatessens, popularly known as delis or sandwich shops, are spreading today like wildfire. With great profit margins and flexibility to adapt and modify menus to meet customer tastes, this is a great option for those who love experimenting and keeping up with the changing trends.

If you are drawn towards smoked and prepared meats, cheeses, salads, and sauces, starting a deli-inspired restaurant may be the perfect option for you. What's more, the idea of a deli is also evolving, with more and more chefs bringing gourmet sensibilities to the humble sandwich, elevating it from just fast food to truly great works of art.

5. Pizzeria

Ask anyone what their favorite pizza is and chances are they'll tell you exactly what toppings they love, the sauce they prefer and even the type of crust right off the top of their head. That's how much pizza has become a part of normal life everywhere around the world. In fact, with different regions laying claim to specific styles of pizza, it has evolved from being an "Italian" dish to something everyone can claim to be their very own.

What's more, you get great flexibility if you're planning on starting a pizzeria. It could either be just focused on the pizza, with minimal fuss and a self-service atmosphere. Or you could go all in and give a complete Italian experience, adding pastas, salads, and other Italian inspired dishes along with your pizzas.

6. Seafood Restaurant

Focused on offering the freshest and best take on seafood, these restaurants are often midscale to upscale and are generally located in places where there is easy access to freshly caught ingredients.

However, as the availability and price of seafood varies based on the season, your business can become quite dependent on what your distributor can offer, making it quite a risky area on which to focus. But if you're truly passionate about seafood and think you want to hero everything beautiful and delicious from the sea this is where you should drop your anchor.

7. Steakhouse

If you are driven by a passion to showcase the best meat prepared in the best possible way, then starting a steak house which focuses exclusively on different cuts of meat is something you'll love. It can either be family-oriented and catered towards larger crowds, where the emphasis is on comfort and hearty food. Or you could start something that is a little more upscale, with decor that leans more towards fine dining establishments with a focus on premium cuts of meat as well as a more private and luxurious ambience.

However, you need to make sure you're an absolute expert when it comes to preparing different cuts of meat, because most of your customers will have a preference in terms of how they like it and the success of a steakhouse pretty much hangs on the ability to serve your customers exactly what they want.

These are just some of the most common food concepts around. If you do your research, you'll realize that the sky's the limit when it comes to how you can tailor your offering and really stand out.

Which leads me to my next point.

What is Your Niche?

So you've decided exactly what type of restaurant you would like to start, the cuisine you want to focus on and the type of customers you would like to attract.

Great!

But depending on the city and area you're planning on setting up your restaurant, there can be anywhere between a handful to more than dozens of restaurants that offer the same cuisine in the same ambience, targeting the exact same audience that you want to bring into your restaurant.

So what can you do to set yourself apart? What can you do to make sure customers choose your restaurant over all these other possible choices they have?

Because if you don't have a niche something that sets you apart from the rest you can guarantee that sooner or later, you will just blend in with the rest of the crowd with nothing to separate you from all the other, similar restaurants around.

Once you've decided exactly what type of restaurant you want to start, you need to take a hard look at your skill set and figure out what skills and techniques you have that can set you apart from the rest. Once you have that list, the next step is to figure out how you can differentiate your offering in terms of ambience, ingredients, and the overall dining experience you can offer to the customers.

Don't worry if some of your ideas seem outlandish. Sometimes, that's what works best.

Just go all out and let your imagination run wild. You will be surprised how much of your own personality you can add into your restaurant and transform something simple and commonplace into a place that truly reflects your passion because in the end, that's all you really need to truly stand out in today's crowded market.

Do You Have a Business Plan?

If you don't, then you really need to get onto it.

While it isn't the most exciting prospect for a chef sitting down to put together a business plan on how and where you see your restaurant going, it is by far the most crucial element of planning your restaurant.

And if you're like most chefs who have been focusing their entire careers only on food, I'm sure you have no clue where to begin.

But that's why you're reading this book, right? So let me help you out.

When you're putting together your restaurant's business plan, here are the most important points to consider and include.

1. A clear definition of your concept
2. Your target market
3. The menu and pricing
4. Detailed financial information, including expense and income forecasts
5. Your marketing plans
6. Employee hiring and training programs

If this all sounds incredibly boring to you, you're not alone. However, if you make sure you get these points exactly right, the journey to your dream restaurant will be that much easier. And once you get there, you'll know exactly how and where everything is going, giving you a clear and precise path to follow towards success.

How Will You Finance It?

Yes, yes. I know.

The boring stuff. And I agree.

No chef wants to think about the finances, especially when that is all that is standing between you and your food dream.

But then again, figuring out how you will finance your restaurant is the 'only' way you will get it off the ground. So might as well dive into it, right?

Now how much money you need to start all depends on a few crucial points. This includes: the style of restaurant, its location, the type of equipment you need, your inventory requirements, your marketing plan, and how much operating capital you will require.

And irrespective of whether you're starting a humble sandwich shop or a sprawling fine dining establishment, you will definitely need to plan your finances to get it up and running not just for a day or a month but for an extensive period of time.

So how do you raise the money you need to get your food dream started? Here are a few suggestions on where you can start.

1. Your own money

> I know, I know. It is highly likely that you don't have a lot of money lying around, definitely not enough to get a restaurant up and running. However, if you're truly determined to pursue your food dream, and you've explored every other option, then maybe it is time to take a loan, max out a few credit cards, and just dive in.
>
> Obviously, this isn't the best or even the most financially efficient way to begin. Neither is this option for everyone. But if all else fails, I say take a leap of faith, put trust in yourself and your abilities and get started.
>
> And if all the money you have in the world is invested in your food dream, you're definitely going to do everything in your power to make it a success, won't you?

2. *Ask friends and family*

When I wanted to stage so I could learn and grow as a chef, my parents played a huge role in making this dream a reality. And if your friends and family truly believe in your skills, passion and drive to succeed, they will definitely be willing to help you out financially in whatever way they can.

However, just because you're approaching people you know and are deeply connected with for finances doesn't mean professionalism goes out the window. Make sure you present yourself, and your business plan, in the most professional way possible. Put everything in writing and give them a clear idea of where the funds will go, as well as a structured plan on how and when they can expect to get their investment back.

3. *Find a partner*

I have had the good fortune of finding someone who truly believes in my vision. And it is that someone who is working hard at making my food dream a reality. Both in terms of finances as well as pushing me forward to help me work at my maximum capability.

Partners come in all shapes and sizes. Some may want to invest in your business while also working side by side with you. Some may just want to invest, with no real interest in dealing with the day-to-day nitty gritty of running a restaurant.

Whatever type of partnership you find, before you sign the dotted line, it is important that you have an iron-clad, written partnership agreement which clearly defines both yours, as well as your partner's obligations and responsibilities in the business.

Another important thing to consider is their outlook. If you and your partner don't really share the same values, it can create huge differences later. And that's the last thing you want when you're trying to take your food establishment to the levels of success of which you've always dreamed.

4. *Explore government programs*

Many countries offer a plethora of programs to support small and medium-sized businesses in getting up and running. If you do your research and find that you qualify for any of these programs, it could go a long way in helping you see your food dream become a reality.

Where Will You Set Up Your Restaurant?

Now you have everything planned. And you even found the perfect way to finance your new venture. It's on to the actual setting up of the restaurant, right?

Not quite yet. There is still one more thing that is left to plan. And this is WHERE you will set up your restaurant.

When it comes to a food establishment, location is everything. It will decide the type of clientele you attract, how much money you will need to procure a place to set up your restaurant, and most importantly, how your establishment is viewed by the general populace. Because more than anything, the right location can give you and your restaurant the sort of image and marketing that money cannot buy.

This means figuring out where you set up your restaurant is one of the most crucial aspects to plan before you actually set out on the road to becoming a restaurant owner. However, with the wide variety of options available, how do you decide which area will be perfect for your future restaurant?

Well, lucky for you, I'm going to list down a few important questions to ask yourself that will give you a lot more clarity regarding where your restaurant should be located.

1. Is the location going to help with your sales volume?

By this I mean you need to find a location which leads to people naturally entering your establishment.

While marketing and word of mouth will definitely help in the long run, when you're starting off, it is of great help if your restaurant is at a location which has a lot of foot traffic meaning people will see your establishment, and hopefully smell the scent of delicious food cooking indoors, drawing them in and creating customers who will come by again and again.

2. *How accessible is it for your customers?*

I cannot tell you the number of restaurants that have failed because they didn't consider one simple aspect when they set up shop at a location parking. Make sure you have plenty of space for potential customers to park, while also making it easily visible and accessible for pedestrians to walk right in without much difficulty.

3. *How much rent can you afford?*

This is where your financial planning comes into play. If you've planned your first year's operating projections, you will have a very clear idea of how much you can afford to pay as rent for your restaurant premises. Needless to say, it is very important to choose a place you can actually afford right away. Because if you rely on sales to bump up your rent-paying capacities, you're just a slow month away from being evicted. And no one wants that.

4. *What other businesses are around?*

If your restaurant is located in an area that has a lot of other businesses that attract people, that is a definite advantage. This means their customers have a higher chance of becoming your customers once they are done with whatever business they were in the area to conduct.

5. *What are the government rules and regulations for the area?*

There are many area rules and regulations that could make an otherwise great option fall flat. Make sure you do your research and find out if there are any restrictive rules and regulations in place that may affect how smoothly your business functions before you settle on location. The last thing you need to find out once your restaurant is up and running is that you can only load or unload your delivery trucks at midnight, and at no other time.

6. *What are the terms offered on your lease?*

A place could be absolutely perfect, but the owner may have terms on the lease that don't sit right with you. In such cases, it is better to move on and find another location rather than finding yourself stuck in a lease agreement that constantly adds more roadblocks to the success of your business.

7. *Are there any future development projects being planned?*

   Maybe you find the perfect spot. It has amazing foot traffic, plenty of parking options, and most importantly, you get a lease with absolutely perfect terms. However, if in a month's time they start construction on a building right next door, you can guarantee that it will have an adverse effect on the business you will attract. That's why it is important to do your research and find out what projects are planned for the future in and around the area before you settle on a location.

Now these questions might not help you nail down the exact spot where your restaurant should stand, but I hope it gives you a clearer idea of what you want from the restaurant location, helping you narrow down a few options from the plethora you will find when you go out there and start looking.

Getting a restaurant up and running isn't an easy business, as I'm sure you've guessed by now. But if you plan smartly and have everything in place before you begin, there is no reason why there should be any obstacle to you realizing your dream of owning your own restaurant.

Chapter 8:
Starting a Restaurant

If you've followed all the steps that I spoke about in the last chapter, then you're well on your way to becoming a restaurant owner.

Your plan is in place. You have all the details sorted out. You're completely confident in your idea. And with all this done, you may believe that the hard work is done, right?

Well, yes and no.

Yes, because once you've put together a foolproof plan, most things will start falling into place. And the difficulties that you will face will be dealt with quickly because you've planned for these contingencies.

No, because actually setting up a restaurant and making it profitable is no easy task either. And no matter how much you plan, no matter how many contingencies you prepare for, there will always be something or the other that will blow you off course.

But I'm here to help break down all the things you need to do, and all the possibilities you can humanly prepare for, so you can make sure such contingencies, and their detrimental effects are minimized as much as possible.

So are you ready to get started?

Then let's jump right in!

Once you've done all the planning, figured out your niche and even found the perfect location to set up your restaurant, the next step is to actually set it up and get it running. But before the first customer even sets foot into your restaurant, you need to figure out what you'll serve them. After all, no matter how amazing your restaurant may look from the outside, the food is always going to be the star. So the next step, and for me the most important, is figuring out your menu.

Creating the Menu

I think it goes without saying that a great menu is the cornerstone of a successful restaurant. After all, people come to restaurants to try something new, something unheard of, or even just a twist on an old classic. And in today's crowded marketplace, your menu is one of the best ways to differentiate yourself from your competitors. So what exactly goes behind creating a great menu? I'm glad you asked.

1. *Design your concept*

    The theme or concept of your restaurant is only effective when it is reflected in your menu. This includes deciding what you want the restaurant to be known for, what flavor profiles you want to highlight and what ingredients you will showcase. The main idea is to offer only those dishes that will really stand out and not clutter your menu with too many items. This will not only help customers easily identify what they would like to order, but will also cause less stress to your kitchen staff and give them the time they need to perfect every single item that is on offer.

2. *Figure out your core ingredients*

Today, the average restaurant goer is a lot more adventurous, which means you can be too with the ingredients you use. It is important to give ingredients a lot of thought, not only making sure they fit within your restaurant concept but also make your customers go wow in terms of. flavors

A great way to keep your ingredient costs down while also ensuring you use the freshest possible ingredients is to use what is easily available nearby such as those in season and those created or offered by artisans in your neighborhood such as cheese and meats. Another aspect that will really help bring your costs down is using ingredients that can be used from top to bottom. This not only sets you apart from a lot of other restaurants but also helps you reduce food costs and wastage.

3. *Plan your supply chain*

The ingredients you plan to use are only as good as the supply chain you put in place. You may have great ideas in terms of the dishes you want to serve to your customers, but if there is an inconsistent supply of the ingredients that make up the dish, then it is going to have a detrimental effect on what you can offer.

The best way to ensure that your supply chain functions smoothly is to connect directly with the supplier. This will ensure that you have a clear idea of what ingredients, and how much of it is available, helping you plan ahead with confidence.

A few key aspects to consider before you choose a supplier include delivery logistics, their storage capabilities as well as the working environment. It is also important that you have at least two to three suppliers for each type of ingredient to ensure that if one falls through, you have backups to keep your restaurant functioning smoothly.

4. *Figure out your costs*

If you have an in-depth business plan in place, you know exactly how much you need to earn in terms of profits to make your restaurant successful. This means you also know exactly how much you need to earn from each dish you serve to your customers.

Figure out how much it will cost to source ingredients and see if it meets your pricing strategy based on your restaurant's location and target audience. A great tool that can help you with this is a recipe management program that will allow you to analyze your menu concept, portions, and cost of ingredients; everything to make sure what you're offering is truly profitable for your restaurant.

5. *Visualize your presentation*

I have seen some great restaurants that serve brilliant food fall behind because of this one simple aspect—

presentation. And presentation is a core part of your restaurant's image.

Figure out how each dish will look on the plate, how the colors work with each other, and in today's social-media driven world, how it will look when photographed. To get a clearer idea, I suggest you plate each dish in multiple ways and see what works best.

6. *Test it out*

As a restaurant owner, you may be too invested in what you want to offer to really have an unbiased opinion on what can work and what won't. That's why it is important to run a few test services where you invite people from your target market and see how they react to the complete package you have to offer. And while the idea of receiving negative feedback even before you're started may seem daunting, trust me when I say that every bit of feedback, negative or positive, will help you start your restaurant on the best foot possible.

If you follow these steps, there is no reason why you can't put together a menu that will help you not only attract the right audience but also ensure that your restaurant is profitable. Just remember that the key is to keep your menu small, offer balanced pricing and only serve what you want to be known for. Once you can figure that out, and put together a concept that sets you apart from your competition, you're well on your way to running a successful restaurant.

Once you have your menu in place, you will get a much clearer idea of how much space you'll need for all the different food items that need to be prepared, as well as your storage requirements. This is also where you focus on your restaurant layout and how it is designed.

Designing the Layout

A restaurant's layout includes many different sections, such as the dining room, kitchen, storage space, and office area. And while designing your restaurant's layout is one of the most important things you need to do to ensure your restaurant's success, a lot of people find it very difficult to figure out. But I'm here to tell you that it doesn't have to be. In fact, once you break down the whole process into a few bite-sized chunks, you'll realize that it is a lot easier than you thought it would be.

So where do you start? Well, which area of the restaurant will make you money? The dining area, of course. And that's where we'll begin.

1. The Dining Room

Now most restaurants tend to allot anywhere between 45 to 65 percent of their restaurant space to the dining area. And when you think about it, that makes a lot of sense doesn't it? The more space you allot to your dining area, the more guests you'll be able to seat, and the more money you will make.

That is also why you should make sure you spend the most amount of time and resources designing this area. While the design and ambience of your dining room will be largely dictated by the type of restaurant you want to start, there is still a lot you can learn by visiting other restaurants in your neighborhood.

See what customers react to when they visit these restaurants. Is there something they seem to absolutely love? Is there something that makes them cringe? By doing this, you will be able to learn from the mistakes other restaurants have made, giving you a leg up before you've even begun.

Another thing to keep in mind while designing your dining area is how you're going to lay out your seating arrangement. There are three major groups of people who will visit your restaurant—people that come in pairs; people that come alone or in groups of three; people who come in larger groups.

Obviously, it is hard to set up your seating in a way where you can cater to all of these groups all of the time. So, the smart thing to do is to use tables for two as much as you can. This means you can just simply push these tables together to accommodate larger groups as and when they come in. What's more, it will also free up a lot of floor space, making it easier for customers as well as your wait staff to walk around, while also giving your dining area the appearance of being larger and roomier than it actually is.

It is a really simple trick; but that's also what makes it so effective.

2. The Production Area

When I say production area, I actually mean a combination of two different sections: the kitchen and the service area. The kitchen, obviously, is the place where all the magic happens. And the service area is where your wait staff will drop off their orders, where all the food will be inspected before it is sent to customers and where the final touches will be made. The kitchen area will also include space where all the food prep will be done.

So when you think production area, you will require space for all of the below:

- Food prep
- Cooking
- Trash storage
- Dishwashing
- Dish storage

A lot of your area requirement also depends on your menu, which means it is important to keep what you are offering in mind while determining each element of your production area.

If you ask a chef how much space should be allotted to this area, you will hear them say the more the better. And that makes sense. Because if you have a small, cramped space where all the cooking and prep is done, you can guarantee that it is going to reflect on the quality of food that comes out. Generally, if you can allot at least 35 percent of your overall layout space to the production area, it works out pretty well. Another important aspect to remember is that everything needs to be within easy reach. The less your chefs and other employees in the kitchen need to move around to get what they need, the faster the entire operation will function. And the quicker your kitchen can send out dishes, the happier your customers will be. See how it is all connected?

3. Storage Area

While your dining area will bring in the money and the production area is where all the magic happens, it is important not to ignore the storage area. Because if you have a well-planned storage area, you will be able to stock up everything you need, while also ensuring there is minimal wastage both of which will help you keep your restaurant ticking like clockwork.

Again, while how much and what type of storage you need depends largely on your menu, there are three major types of storage area that most restaurants require.

- Dry Storage

For items and ingredients that don't require specific temperature and climate-controlled environments, dry storage is where they will go. This is where items that generally have a longer shelf-life, such as flour, sugar, grains and canned goods, are kept. And because this area does not require any specific climate controls, it is much easier to maintain as well.

- Refrigerated Storage

As the name implies, refrigerated storage is where food items are kept that need to be stored at cool temperatures so that they remain fresh and do not go bad.

Cheeses, meats, seafood, butter, vegetables and eggs are just some of the many food items that are kept in refrigerated storage. It is very important that the right temperature is maintained in this area at all times. This doesn't just reduce wastage of food due to spoilage, but also prevents contamination which can result in your restaurant patrons falling ill, and that is one of the worst things that can happen to a restaurant, especially one that is just starting off.

- Frozen Storage

Frozen storage is used for when you want your fresh ingredients to stay fresh for longer. This is also where costly ingredients such as essences, processed foods such as fruit juices and pulp, as well as frozen meat, seafood and dairy is stored. And when it comes to the temperature, just like refrigerated storage, it is important that the right temperature is maintained at all times to prevent spoilage and contamination of food.

Another important aspect to remember about food storage is the 'First In, First Out' concept. This basically means that everything should be stored in such a way that the oldest addition is always used first, ensuring that there is minimum wastage because it does not exceed its use-by date, while also ensuring food safety as there is a reduced chance of spoilage.

4. *Office Space*

The last, but not the least, because you will end up spending a lot of time here trust me, I know it is the office space. Now the priority should always be given to all the other areas of the restaurant, and I think that goes without saying. However, the office space should be large enough that you have space to store all the required documentation, while also not being so cramped that being in there seems like a punishment.

As I mentioned, you will be spending a lot of time here, so it is important to make sure it is comfortable enough that you can spend hours without feeling trapped or claustrophobic. Additionally, it is quite possible you will meet your business contacts here as well. So decorating it to give just the right impression is also necessary.

Another addition that I generally add into the office space is a place for your employees to chance. You cannot expect your chefs or wait staff to travel from wherever they live to your restaurant dressed in uniform. By giving them an area where they can change into their uniforms, you also give them a space they can duck into when they need a breather. And they will need it, especially once your restaurant is so popular that people keep coming in through the doors.

While there may be other areas you need to account for when setting up your restaurant depending on the style and type of place you aim to create, if you account for these three major areas, I believe you will have a strong foundation on which to start.

Now that you've decided what you're going to serve and how your restaurant is going to be laid out, let us discuss how people will perceive your restaurant. And for that, you need to give a lot of attention to how your dining area is planned and designed. While we have already discussed how you can lay out your tables to optimally utilize your dining area space, there are other aspects that you need to consider that will help you bring your restaurant concept to life and truly wow your guests. And that is how you decorate your dining area, because that is what sets the tone and ambience of your restaurant more than anything else.

To help you along and give you the best possible start, here are a few tips that I have learned over the years.

1. Space is important

It is easy to want to put as many tables and chairs as you can in your dining area. After all, the more the number of people you can seat the more profitable you will be, right? Possibly, but that also means creating a cramped dining space where your customers feel claustrophobic and get absolutely no privacy.

As I mentioned earlier, the best way to approach this is by setting up as many two-seater options as possible, which not only leaves adequate space between tables, but also lets you accommodate larger crowds by moving these tables together as and when required.

2. Personally try out every seating option

There is no better way to get a customer's perspective on seating options than sitting on them yourself and experiencing exactly what they would experience. Some seating options may directly be in the way of a draft, or some may have a view of the kitchen as the doors open and close. By making sure you take in the seating experience, you can prepare for any potential customer complaints and make changes before that even happens.

3. *Get the furniture right*

While your tables and chairs form a key part of your restaurant experience, you also need to account for how much time and effort will go behind cleaning and wiping them down. Intricate designs and carvings will only make it harder to get into all the crevices, which means longer cleaning times.

Additionally, if your furniture is not sturdy, you may need to replace them more than you want. And that is going to make your overall costs shoot up. This means, it is better to spend a little extra and go for something that will last for longer than skimp out and end up paying more because you have to keep replacing the furniture you buy.

4. *Create the right playlist*

Music plays an important role in setting the mood and ambience in your restaurant. So make sure you spend enough time deciding the genre and curating a playlist of music that will help set the right tone.

Another important aspect to consider is the volume at which the music will be playing. If it is a bar or something more casual, louder music is tolerated or even expected. But if you're trying to create a cozy ambience, a much quieter setting will definitely be better.

5. *Choose the perfect colors*

The effect of colors on our moods has been well documented. So do a little research and see which colors will work best with the ambience you're trying to create. Bright colors such as red give the impression of a fun, lively place, while lighter colors such as blue create a calm and soothing environment. Another thing to remember here is the type of window coverings you use. If your restaurant takes in direct sunlight during the day, you may want to invest in drapes that will keep the sun out while ensuring the insides get enough daylight. This won't just create a better ambience but will also reduce your cooling costs.

I'm sure you're thinking that now, after all this, you should be finally able to open your restaurant to customers, right? You could, but you will also be shut down just as soon. Why? Because of the most important, albeit boring, thing that you forgot getting the necessary licenses.

Depending on the type of restaurant you want to open and the country you're opening it in, there are a plethora of licenses you need that show that your restaurant complies with all the health and safety codes that are in place. Here are some of the most common licenses restaurants need.

1. Trade License
2. Food Safety License
3. Tax Registration
4. Business Registration

5. Liquor License

The costs of these vary from country to country, and may even vary between different regions within the same country. I suggest you get started on the application process as early as possible so nothing comes in the way once you've got everything else in place. And keep in mind that in certain countries it may take a lot longer to get these licenses than others so plan accordingly.

Finally, it is time to say congratulations!

You now have everything in place to open your doors and let the customers start flooding into your new restaurant.

But what is this? Not seeing a lot of footfalls?

Maybe that's because you haven't marketed your restaurant, or not marketed it well.

Don't worry. I can help you out.

1. Make use of social media

This seems like a no-brainer but there are a lot of restaurants that purely depend on word-of-mouth and old-school marketing, completely forgetting about leveraging social media to their best advantage. Creating social media handles for your restaurant on all the popular channels is the best way to communicate your restaurant's brand, the food you have to offer and give your customers a peek into the experience they can expect when they step through your restaurant's doors.

Take plenty of videos, especially behind-the-scenes, get a professional food photographer to take delicious and mouthwatering pictures of your dishes and actively engage with your target audience on every channel. Once you get this going, sooner or later you will have a dedicated following online, which in turn will translate into more and more customers lining up outside to get a taste of what you have to offer.

It is also a great way to communicate any offers or specials you may have that set you apart from the rest, giving you a great platform to stand out from the rest of your competition.

2. *Create a great website*

Your website is a window into your restaurant. It not just makes you and your restaurant seem a lot more professional and well-established, it also acts as a place where potential customers can get answers to the questions they have that might be keeping them from actually visiting your restaurant.

It also acts as a great way for potential customers to find you while they are surfing the web, and if you really focus on getting your content and keywords right, your website and in turn your restaurant, will start popping up on your target audience's screen whenever they search for any terms that connect with your restaurant.

3. *Don't hold back on offers*

No matter how great your food is, sometimes the only push a potential customer need is a great deal. Create themed offers on relevant days, such as Christmas and Valentine's Day, and get those hesitant customers to make the decision to come in through your doors.

And once they are there, you can trust your food and ambience to do the rest, converting a first-time customer into someone who will keep visiting for years to come.

4. Get the competitive spirit going

What people like more than offers is the chance to win something, and this is also a great way to get word-of-mouth going. Offering contests is a great way to get customers, existing and potential, to interact with your brand in your restaurant and online, increasing how far and wide your restaurant's name spreads.

5. Tie up with bloggers and influencers

When you're starting off, your online presence may not have the reach you really need to give your restaurant's foot traffic that you are aiming for with your online communication. At this point, it is a great idea to tie up with influencers and food bloggers who already have a huge following, leveraging their reach to get your restaurant's visibility to a much larger audience.

6. Work on your online reputation

More often than not, a potential customer will go through multiple online reviews before they decide whether your restaurant is worth visiting. And I don't need to tell you about horror stories where even a single bad review has ended up tanking a restaurant's otherwise stellar reputation.

Make sure you respond to all online customer queries as soon as possible, as well as engaging with customers who leave reviews positive or negative. Especially the negative ones. This will make your brand come across as approachable, creating a better reputation overall.

7. *Get an expert*

If you think you, or your team, doesn't really have the right know-how to get your marketing up and running, it is always better to get a professional or a team of professionals to help you out.

After all, it is better to have the best start to your marketing rather than have to go back and course correct once you realize your efforts are being put in the wrong direction. This means putting together a team that really knows how to market, especially online, and get it right the first time around. You won't regret it.

A word of advice: while all of these are great ways to market your restaurant and spread your brand name far and wide, if what you're actually offering at your restaurant both in terms of food and the ambience lags behind, then marketing is not really going to help you.

So before you even start figuring out how you want to market what you're offering, you should firmly focus on what you're offering. And if your food and ambience really stands out, marketing is only going to help further.

Now I will be the first to admit that there are a lot of other ways you can market your restaurant, especially in today's ever-evolving digital space. But if you start off by focusing on these few areas, there is no reason why your brand, and your restaurant, can't have the best start right from the beginning.

Chapter 9: Making Your Restaurant Profitable

Congratulations!

Your new restaurant is now off the ground. Your social media is on point. You're getting rave reviews.

But just because customers are pouring in doesn't mean your restaurant has achieved the levels of profitability that it can. In fact, I can guarantee that if you don't really focus on increasing profitability in various areas, once the initial burst dies out, you'll find it hard to keep your restaurant as profitable as it was when it started off.

So how can you make your restaurant profitable so it can continue growing and expanding? I'm glad you asked, because there are three areas where, if you put in time and energy, you can truly take your restaurant's profitability to the next level. These are:

1. Costs and Profit Margin
2. Sourcing
3. Technology

Costs and Profit Margin

Costs

Most restaurant owners will tell you that controlling costs is the most challenging aspect of running a restaurant. They are not wrong. There are labor costs, equipment costs, supply costs. And over a period of time, these costs only go up.

That's why the first step to increasing profitability is to understand where you're actually spending your money, and how you can optimize these costs to get the best results. But before you even get started on optimizing your expenditure, it is important to understand what exactly it means, and the different types of costs you will encounter.

Now before we begin, I want to clarify that there is a difference between restaurant expenses and costs. While restaurant costs are primarily a one-time expenditure, such as dishes or equipment, restaurant expenses are recurring payments such as rent, payroll, or marketing expenditure. Your costs are then further split into fixed costs and variable costs. Fixed costs are easier to budget because they don't tend to vary from period to period and include rent, salaries, mortgage, and license fees. Your variable costs, on the other hand, are harder to predict as they vary according to your output, and you'll only get a clearer idea of these as your restaurant continues functioning for a few months.

Apart from these, there is also prime cost, which is the sum of *Direct Labor Costs and Costs of Goods Sold (which includes employee benefits, payroll taxes, healthcare, and bonuses).*

This is a great indicator of your restaurant's performance, and also has the biggest impact on your restaurant's profitability. There are a few reasons why:

1. These will be your largest restaurant expenses.
2. They will change constantly, which means they require constant monitoring and tracking.
3. They affect almost every aspect of your restaurant.

I know it sounds a little complicated, so let me break it down for you.

Prime Costs = Cost of Goods Sold + Total Labor Cost

Here's how you calculate your Cost of Goods Sold:

Cost of Goods Sold = Beginning Inventory of F&B + Purchases – End Inventory

So, if your beginning inventory for a particular month is $10,000, you bought inventory worth $5,000 and your inventory at the end of the month is $7,000, then your Cost of Goods Sold is $8,000 ($10,000 + 5,000 – 7,000)

Then you calculate your total labor cost for the same period:

Total Labor Cost = Salaries for the period + Total wages of hourly workers

So if your monthly salaries are $5,000 and wages are $5,000, then your Total Labor Cost for the month is $10,000.

And once you have both these numbers, calculating your Prime Cost is easy. Just add your Cost of Goods Sold and Total Labor Cost.

So your Cost of Goods sold for the above example will be $18,000 ($8,000 + $10,000)

However, just having your Prime Cost number really doesn't offer you much insight. Where it really helps is when calculated as percentage of sales.

This is how you get there.

Prime Cost Percentage = Prime Cost ÷ Total Sales

So if your Prime Cost is $18,000 as per the above example and your earnings from your sales or Total Sales is $36,000, then your Prime Cost Percentage is 50% of your sales earnings. This means you use 50% of your earnings to cover your expenses. And needless to say, the lower your Prime Cost Percentage, the more profitable your restaurant will be.

But how do you bring down your Prime Cost Percentage? For that, you need to focus on four major restaurant costs that you will encounter:

1. Labor costs

> I think we can all agree that no restaurant can function without a labor force. But this is also an area where you need a substantial amount of investment. And the best way to ensure that your labor costs don't spiral out of control is by managing them better.
>
> Your first instinct when it comes to controlling your labor costs may be to cut down on staff or keep them on reduced hours. While these steps may reduce your labor costs, it can also have an adverse effect on the

overall quality of customer service, which in turn is going to negatively affect your profits making the entire process counterintuitive.

Instead of cutting down on staff, here are three steps you can take to reduce your labor costs without having a detrimental effect on your service quality or your profits:

- **Give staff the best training you can**

The better training the members of your staff get, the more efficient they will be. This means you will be able to get a lot more done, that too a lot quicker, without it having a negative impact on your quality of service.

- **Focus on improving employee retention**

Needless to say, happy employees are the best employees. And a great indicator of how happy your employees are is your employee turnover. Training new employees is one of the biggest drains on your resources in terms of time and money. And the higher your employee turnover, the more you will end up spending on new hires.

This means holding on to your employees, especially the best ones, is one of the most important things to focus on. Rewarding your best employees as well as providing them growth opportunities are just two of the many ways in which you can improve employee morale, and in turn, employee retention.

- **Optimize employee scheduling**

As a restaurant owner, it is easy to lose track of employee scheduling amongst all the other aspects of running a restaurant that need your attention. However, under-scheduling and over-scheduling can both increase your labor costs, which means getting your scheduling absolutely right can make all the difference to your profitability.

2. *Utility Costs*

Now utility costs, which include water, electricity, gas, internet, and mobile phone costs are something that will vary from restaurant to restaurant depending on multiple factors such as location, size, and even the weather. And while you can't always cut down these costs, there are a couple of ways in which you can optimize them and keep them in check.

- **Manage your consumption**

This seems like a no-brainer but you will be surprised at how many restaurants end up facing huge utility bills because they don't optimize their consumption of utilities. Just by using something as simple as energy saving bulbs or energy efficient appliances can make all the difference to your utility costs.

- **Put on your negotiation hat**

    Many utility providers, especially internet and mobile phone service providers, will be willing to provide cheaper rates if you negotiate package deals with them for your restaurant as well as your staff. Yes, they may ask for the payments to be made upfront, but if you can reduce your overall utility costs this way, it is only going to have a positive impact on your profitability.

3. *Kitchen Equipment Costs*

    Your kitchen equipment costs include everything from furniture and small utensils to big items such as ovens and cooking ranges. Here again, the size and concept of your restaurant will have a huge impact on your kitchen equipment costs, which also include the cost of repairing or replacing anything that breaks down. There are many ways in which you can reduce your equipment costs:

- **Lease what you need**

    When you're starting off, kitchen equipment costs, especially for some of the bigger and more expensive ones can be prohibitive. In such scenarios, leasing can be a great option, where you make monthly payments for the equipment you need, and that's it.

- **Get regular maintenance done**

    A lot of kitchen equipment, like ovens and refrigerators, need to be serviced regularly to keep them running optimally. This doesn't just reduce the utility cost as they will use less electricity or gas, but they will also break down less, saving you repair costs, or even the cost of replacing equipment regularly.

- **Reduce breakages**

    Glasses and plates will break. You might as well get used to the idea. But if you have well-trained staff as well as proper storage areas for everything fragile, you will see a lot less breakage, which in turn reduces the amount you will spend each month on replacing the broken items.

4. **Food Costs**

Needless to say, this is the most important cost you should be tracking and optimizing if you want your restaurant to be profitable. The more optimized your food costs, the more your profits, and there are a few strategies you can use to make sure these costs stay low right from the start.

- **Minimize food wastage**

  A lot of restaurants end up throwing away sections of ingredients they don't use. This wastage of food isn't just bad from a moral standpoint, but can also make your costs shoot up drastically. Figure out ways in which you can use as much of a particular ingredient as possible so you can minimize food wastage, and in turn your food costs.

- **Optimize your portion sizes**

  Are your restaurant patrons sending plates back with food leftover on a regular basis? Then maybe it is time you rethink your portion sizes. Large portion sizes may seem generous, but if they are more than what your average customer consumes, you are better off serving smaller portions which will also help you cut down on your food costs.

- **Have more than one supplier**

  Different suppliers may quote different prices for the same ingredient due to a variety of reasons. If you maintain a good relationship with multiple suppliers, you will be able to pick and choose from one who gives you the best rate, helping you keep down your supply costs.

- **Manage your inventory**

    Food wastage due to spoilage can be a huge issue for a restaurant, and it most likely indicates a problem with your inventory management system. If your restaurant loses ingredients to spoilage regularly, it may be time to relook how you're managing your inventory.

These are just some of the few areas where if you can manage to keep your costs down, you should be able to increase the profitability of your restaurant. However, there is another way to look at your restaurant's profitability, and that's by focusing on your profit margin.

Profit Margin

Before we get into how you can increase your restaurant's profit margins, I want to help you distinguish between the two types of profit margins we will be discussing.

The first is *Gross Profit*, which is the difference between the selling price of your dish and the cost of ingredients that are used to make the dish.

The second is *Net Profit* , which is the Gross Profit with operating expenses such as rent, utility bills, and equipment leasing costs deducted from it.

Simple to understand right? Then let's move on to the important stuff.

So how can you improve your restaurant's profit margin? Broadly speaking, there are two primary ways you can do so: increase your sales volume and decrease your overhead expenses. And while there are many ways you can do both, here I'm going to share some easy to execute methods that you can start using in your restaurant right away.

Let's jump right in.

1. Increasing Sales Volume

This makes sense, right? The more you sell, the more you earn and the higher your profits. Not really rocket science. But how do you sell more? By selling more, I don't mean dragging customers through the front door that's for your marketing team to worry about. Here, by selling more I mean getting customers who are already in your restaurant to spend more, thereby increasing the sales you generate per table.

And to increase sales volume, there are three main pillars on which you need to focus:

- **Work on your dish pricing**

    The first, and the easiest, way to increase your profit margin is to optimize the prices of your dishes. And for that, you need to know how to calculate two aspects of every dish: your cost per serving and the food cost percentage.

    Yes, we're going back to some mathematics, but trust me when I say these can make all the difference to your restaurant's profit margin. So stay with me.

    Your cost per serving is the cost of a single dish, and while calculating it may be a little harder than, let's say calculating food costs for the entire restaurant, with a little bit of thought and ingenuity, it is quite possible to come up with a number. So how do you calculate your cost per serving? We can break it down to three steps:

Step 1: List out all the ingredients, along with the proportion or weight of ingredients used,

Step 2: Now determine the cost of the proportion of ingredients used in the dish. This is where it gets a little complicated, so let me give you an example. Let's say from 1 kilogram of rice, you can get 50 portions. This means, to get the cost of rice in one serving, you need to divide the total cost of rice by 50 servings, and there you have it.

Step 3: Once you have the cost of all the ingredients that go into one serving, the final step is add all of them together and you will get your cost per serving.

From the cost per serving, getting to your food cost percentage is simple. Just divide your *Cost Per Serving* by the *Menu Price of the Dish* and *multiply by 100* or:

Food Cost Percentage = (Cost Per Serving ÷ Menu Price) x 100

Once you have your food cost percentage, you will get a much clearer idea of whether your dish is underpriced or overpriced. A general rule of thumb that is used in most restaurants is that if the food cost percentage is above 30-35 percent, the dish is underpriced, which means you can and should raise the menu price of that dish until your food cost percentage drops to this range.

By doing this, you will ensure that you are making the most amount of profit from every single dish, thereby increasing your profit margin. And if you're worried about scaring away customers by suddenly increasing your prices, I suggest you do that subtly over a period of time so it is not such a sudden change for your customers. Or you can increase profit margins by reducing your cost of ingredients. Just make sure you don't do so by compromising on the quality of ingredients or you'll soon start losing customers.

- **Optimize what's on your menu**

    When you start your restaurant, there will be a lot of dishes that you want to showcase for a plethora of different reasons. Some may be your favorite and some may have ingredients you want to champion or some may just be what you personally love to cook. However, once you actually start serving customers you will realize that some dishes are not as popular as others, while others are not as profitable. By optimizing your menu to only include your most popular dishes which are also the most profitable, you can make sure that no matter what a customer orders, it is good for your profit margin. At the same time, by removing the dishes that are not as profitable, you get the chance to add on new dishes which earn you a higher profit margin than the ones you took off.

So how do you figure out which are your most popular and profitable dishes? Here's how:

Step 1: Analyze your sales

Go through your restaurant's sales reports and figure out which dishes are popular or unpopular, and which ones are more profitable than others.

Step 2: Categorize your dishes

Break down your menu items into four categories based on their profitability and popularity.

Category 1: High Profitability, High Popularity
These are the stars of your restaurant and should be featured prominently on your menu.

Category 2: High Profitability, Low Popularity
These may need to be rethought or may need a push from your waitstaff.

Category 3: Low Profitability, High Popularity
These are popular items that your customers know and love already.

Category 4: Low Profitability, Low Popularity
These items may need to be rethought or repriced, or you may want to replace them with other dishes.

Step 3: Rework your menu

The first thing you need to do once you figure out your least profitable and popular dishes is to phase these out and replace them with dishes that are more profitable. Once you're done this, the next step is to rework your menu to highlight your most profitable dishes in such a way that more customers pay attention to them and order them.

- **Focus on table turnover**

    So what exactly is Table Turnover? The term refers to the amount of time a guest, or a group of guests, spends at a table in your restaurant, calculated from the moment they enter till they leave. Now it goes without saying that the more the number of guests you serve during a service, the more revenue you earn. But how do you maximize your table turnover, and in turn, your revenue per table during service?

You obviously cannot rush your customers, but at the same time, you don't want them to linger around after their meal is done, because that means you lose time, as well as money, that another set of guests could be spending.

To find the right balance and increase your table turnover, here areas on which you should focus:

Area 1: Seating guests

It goes without saying that the faster you seat guests, the quicker you will be able to serve them. And the best way to make sure your guests are seated as soon as possible and avoid any bottlenecks at your front door is to make sure your host, who will be the first person our guests interact with, is quick and efficient. If your restaurant doesn't have a host, I suggest you look into it as it can make all the difference in how quickly guests are greeted and seated once they enter your restaurant.

Area 2: Serving guests

Once your guests are seated, the next step is actually serving them. And the biggest factor that influences how quickly your wait staff can serve a table is the amount of time it takes them to write down an order and then pass it on to the kitchen. Well-trained wait staff will work in perfect harmony with the kitchen staff, passing on orders in a clear and precise manner. Needless to say, the more they are in sync, the faster you will be able to serve your guests.

Area 3: Processing Payments

Your guests were seated and served in record time. Great! But once they are done, if you take too long to bring them their bill and process their payment, then all that efficiency goes to wait. That's why the final area on which you should focus to increase table turnover times is how quickly you can process customer payments.

All this extra attention to detail doesn't just increase table turnovers. It also communicates to your customers that you are running an efficient and well-oiled business, giving them yet another reason to come again this time with other guests perhaps.

2. Decreasing Overhead Expenses

While increasing your revenue is a great way to make your restaurant more profitable, there will come a point where you will feel there are no other avenues through which you can keep doing so, at least without losing out on customers. That's why, focusing on decreasing your overhead expenses is another great viewpoint through which you can increase your net revenue, and in turn your restaurant's profitability.

Now I know what you must be thinking. How do you even go about decreasing your overheads if you planned everything down to the last penny? Well, if you look close enough, there are always areas where you can cut down, even a little bit. And it's these little cuts that will make all the difference in the long run. The three main areas where you can start focusing to reduce your overhead expenses are:

- **Employee scheduling**

    Every restaurant has an ebb and flow of customers times when there are always more customers coming through the door and times when there will be fewer of them. And if you end up scheduling more staff when your restaurant isn't as busy, you could spend too much on labor costs. At the same time, if you schedule less staff during your peak hours, you could end up slowing down table turnover rates which, as we discussed, will end up eating into your profit margin.

    This means, optimal employee scheduling can make all the difference to your overhead costs if you plan them according to when it is the busiest, and the slowest, in your restaurant. So your goal is to schedule the right number of staff to meet customer demands at any point during the day. Once you get employee scheduling right, it is a great way to increase revenue and decrease your overheads, without negatively impacting the service and food you offer.

- **Food waste**

We've discussed this at length earlier, so I won't go into this point in much detail. But as mentioned earlier, food waste plays a huge role in upping your overheads. And if you really focus on keeping any such waste to a minimum, there is no reason why your profitability shouldn't go up.

- **Utility bills**

Restaurants, in general, consume a lot more energy than other commercial establishments; this is common knowledge. Which automatically means that your utility bills will be high. But in today's world where technology has come such a long way, there is one big step you can take to minimize your energy footprint investing in energy efficient appliances.

Yes, the initial cost of these appliances can be steep. However, the long-term effects energy saving appliances have is immense, ensuring that you can save on your utility bills over the years, reducing your overheads quite a bit.

I've said it before and I'll say it again there is no "one way" to increase your profit margins that will work for every restaurant. However, these are a few tried and tested steps you can take immediately and see how it impacts your profits helping you be on your way to running a profitable restaurant.

Sourcing

Margins in the restaurant business have never been lower. And with more and more customers questioning the choice to eat outside on a regular basis as their own expenses rise, restaurants themselves face an overwhelming need to reduce prices further lowering these margins.

So how can you, as a restaurant owner, work towards reducing the pressure to cut costs in places that may be detrimental to your final output, while also maintaining profitability? Other than the myriad of areas we already discussed, there is one important aspect of the restaurant business that many first-time restaurateurs ignore. And that is sourcing.

By really taking stock of your expenses, and challenging suppliers to provide the lowest costs possible, you can optimize your sourcing strategy and ensure you get the best value possible. Value that you can also pass on to your customers making them even happier with what you have to offer.

Sounds easier said than done? Not really! Let me show you how.

1. Create a sourcing strategy

The restaurant business has long worked on relationships. This means if you feel that a long-time supplier is providing a fair cost and makes deliveries on time, this means there is no need to really go out there and look for other options. And if going out there and looking for more options ruins an existing relationship, that's not worth it either. Right?

Well, not if you want to run a profitable restaurant. In fact, you could lose out on a lot of earnings if you continue working with a particular supplier if there are alternatives that could give you a much higher profitability benefit.

It is important to remember that the lowest cost a supplier can realistically offer will always be lower than what you think it should be. This means there is always wriggle-room to negotiate further. And if this can help you increase your profit margins even by the tiniest sliver, it can make all the difference in the long run.

So do your research and really understand the true costs of everything you source. Then go to your existing supplier and lay down your expectations. And if you feel those are not met, don't hesitate to look for other options. After all, no one is more dedicated to increasing your restaurant's profitability than you.

2. *Source local*

A lot of restaurants are making a shift towards sourcing and working with local, seasonal ingredients across the world. And for good reason.

It not only offers restaurants a chance to offer dishes prepared with the freshest ingredients as well as an opportunity to promote and support other local establishments, it also provides a cheaper alternative to sourcing ingredients from far away areas helping you avoid excessive costs related to transportation and storage, among others.

As well as providing you with a cheaper alternative for ingredients, it also helps build goodwill for your business in the locality—and you can't put a price on the resultant positive word-of-mouth you will generate.

3. *Schedule quarterly meetings*

Costs fluctuate regularly, especially when it comes to the restaurant business. This means, the deal you have agreed upon last quarter may not be profitable this quarter. By ensuring that you meet your suppliers quarterly and re-examine where you stand, you will be able to stay on top of fluctuating prices and get the best possible deal.

Another benefit of quarterly meetings is that you will be able to plan ahead for every quarter effectively, in terms of cost as well as what you need, making sure you have a crystal-clear plan of action for the coming months that is not weighed down by uncertainties.

4. *Explore other categories*

When you think of sourcing, you think of ingredients, right? After all, that is the major aspect you need to figure, and put in place, so your restaurant functions smoothly on a day-to-day basis. However, there are other avenues that you should consider where sourcing relationships can be built which will help you reduce your overall costs, both direct and indirect, resulting in higher overall profitability.

A few categories that you can consider for sourcing are health insurance, decorating, and telecom. By keeping track of your expenses in these categories, reviewing them and finding new alternatives that could possibly provide you with lower rates will keep your restaurant competitive, positively impacting your end profit margin.

5. *Bring on a professional*

A lot of restaurateurs will tell you that they want, in fact need, to be the ones handling all the work that goes behind sourcing. However, there are a plethora of experts in the field who, with their years of experience, are much better equipped to find the best available options and negotiate the lowest available rates.

After all, the rigors of running a restaurant aren't for the faint hearted. And if you can find an expert whose opinion you can trust, delegating this task to them can really increase your profit margins to a level that you thought was unimaginable.

Yes, it may need a little bit of investment in the beginning which may not really reflect in your profitability from the start. But what such a professional will bring to the table will far outweigh the cost you will incur by bringing them onboard especially in the long run.

These are just some of the ways you can increase your profitability by reworking and rethinking the way you look at your current sourcing methods. But if you truly want to transform your restaurant's profitability, the best way to approach it is by adopting technology. And with the way technology has evolved over the last few years, everything, from sourcing to scheduling has been made easy allowing you to focus on what truly needs your attention in the restaurant and delegating what doesn't to the options offered by today's technology.

Technology

As I mentioned, there is no shortage of restaurant technology aimed at helping increase operational efficiency and customer experience, and in turn, profitability. In fact, many restaurants are incorporating technology into their operations to such an extent that there is barely any human involvement at all, from the cash register to the kitchen.

You've all seen videos of restaurants run completely by robots, right?

While such a restaurant is still something that only truly works in a science fiction movie, there are many ways in which you can incorporate technology into your restaurant right away that will make running it easier, faster, and more profitable. Here, I will talk about a few areas where technology can be incorporated effortlessly, technology that has already proven to have a positive impact not only to a restaurant's profitability, but also to the overall customer experience and satisfaction.

1. Scheduling

We have already discussed how important optimizing scheduling is to your restaurant's profitability. Having the right number of staff at the right time can have a huge impact on your profit margins, while also playing an important role in a customer's overall experience at your restaurant. But I'm sure every restaurateur who has been in the business for a while will agree when I say that creating an optimal schedule that takes every single variable into account, such as holidays, area foot traffic or even the weather is next to impossible. So how do you make sure you optimize your staff schedule? With the right technology, of course.

Today, there are plenty of software tailored specifically to help restaurants optimize their scheduling, getting the job done effectively and efficiently in a fraction of the time. These software's take a plethora of variables into account, including historical staffing patterns, forecasted sales, staff performance, employee availability, and even the weather. In fact, most also monitor sales and staffing budgets to automatically control and reduce overtime, further positively impacting your restaurant's profitability.

This means, you not only get the right people at the right place at the right time, but you do all that while ensuring that your profit margins are not affected.

2. Inventory

Managing inventory to ensure you have the right amount of everything you need at all times can be difficult. If you have too much of something, you have money tied up in things or ingredients you don't require. And if you have too little of it, it adversely affects how smoothly your restaurant functions. However, with the advent in technology, personally managing inventory on a day-to-day basis is a thing of the past.

Today, most restaurants use a digital inventory system that, through a simple mobile device, allows you and your employees to monitor inventory at all times, while also allowing for requests for new additions to be made within minutes. What's more, certain inventory software can even predict future inventory requirements using recipe and point of sale data, calculating the amount of inventory you need to have on hand.

Such software can greatly increase inventory management efficiency and accuracy, reducing loss due to over-ordering, under-ordering or wastage keeping you on top of your inventory requirements at all times.

3. Purchasing

One of the biggest nightmare scenarios for a restaurant owner is to not have food to serve a customer. But when you have an automated purchasing tool connected to your inventory management system that alerts you when inventory is running low, you can rest assured that such a scenario will never materialize.

Such a purchasing tool can take a plethora of variables into consideration, including supplier delivery times and forecasted sales quantities, while also allowing you to enable automatic purchase requests that will be placed to suppliers when inventory levels reach a certain limit.

This means you can automate your entire purchasing process, from approving orders to creating invoices, allowing you to give your entire attention to other, more pressing aspects of running a restaurant.

4. Staff and Kitchen Communication

Fast food restaurants have already embraced technology when it comes to the ordering process. Today, customers can browse the menu, customize their orders and even pay for their meals, everything on a single tablet without a single human in sight. While it may be more beneficial for fast food outlets at the moment, using technology that transmits a customer's order from the wait staff to the kitchen as soon as it is noted down on the staff's tablet can make a huge difference in terms of accuracy of the order.

It also reduces the time taken for the order to be conveyed to the kitchen, which only further helps increase table turnover. And this, as we discussed, is one of the most important parameters to increase your restaurant's profitability.

Additionally, it communicates the status of a customer's order to the wait staff in real time, so they can update the customer and give them the exact time when they expect their order to come to their table, down to the minute.

5. Reservations

If you ask customers what they hate most about going to a restaurant, waiting for a table will be on top of their list. But if you have a digital table manager in place that handles everything from taking booking reservations to suggesting seating based on time and size of the group, you can rest assured that your customer experience is going to be nothing but exemplary, at least when it comes to making reservations. In fact, reservation software even automatically communicates any wait times that a customer may expect much in advance via text, ensuring that they can plan their commute accordingly and not have to wait outside the restaurant for even a single minute.

6. Home delivery

We've all used the plethora of applications that are available through which we can place delivery orders in seconds, without needing any sort of human interference. And embracing such technology is not only beneficial to the customer, but also to the restaurant itself.

Not only does it eliminate the need for a member of the staff to monitor the phones just to take down orders, many companies who manage such applications also offer their own delivery services to areas which may be outside your own coverage area. Or maybe you don't offer the option for home delivery at all. By leveraging the delivery opportunity offered by such applications, you can not only add to the sales you make already by serving customers who come to your restaurant, you don't even need to invest in your own delivery staff.

Additionally, it gives you the best opportunity to reach a larger customer base with minimal marketing, many of whom may actually become regulars to your restaurant, making a positive impact to your profitability not just for a short period of time, but in the long run as well.

A lot to take in, isn't it?

I'm sure it is. However, within this exhaustive list of ways to increase a restaurant's profitability, I'm sure you will find suggestions that will have an impact on your specific restaurant no matter what type it is.

The idea is to constantly try new avenues for growth, allowing your restaurant and how it functions to evolve with the changing trends. At the same time, by focusing on the basics, and really getting all the small details to work for you. You can transform your restaurant from something that is simply profitable, to a huge success.

Chapter 10: Growing Your Restaurant

You've been a restaurant owner for a while now. The initial struggles of setting up your first restaurant and getting it going are long forgotten. You now have a loyal following and regular clientele, ensuring that your venture works pretty much on its own at this point of time.

What next?

If you've been running a successful restaurant for a while, I'm sure the most common suggestion you would have received from customers is they wish you had a branch that was closer to where they stay.

That gets you thinking, doesn't it?

Maybe it is time to spread your wings and look into expanding your restaurant into a chain serving a much wider audience and spreading the brand name far and wide.

And considering how you've already done such a great job with your first restaurant, you're much better prepared this time around for anything the process can throw at you. That should make expanding easy, right?

Yes, and no.

Yes, you understand the process much better and can prepare for most of the uncertainties that come with opening a new restaurant.

No, because no matter how many restaurants you open, there is no guarantee the next one will be as successful as the one before. And trust me when I say that somehow, every new restaurant opening brings its own set of unique issues that you could never have imagined.

That doesn't mean you should hesitate from taking that next step expanding your restaurant into a chain. But before you do, there are two questions you need to ask yourself before you embark on this journey of expansion.

First, is your restaurant concept genuinely scalable?

As a first-time restaurant owner, you need to understand that the concept of scalability is one of the most important factors that determines the success of your restaurant chain. And as hard as it may be to admit, not every restaurant concept is scalable. The more niche or complex your concept, the less likely it is to succeed as a chain.

Second, are you mentally, emotionally, and financially equipped to tackle the enormous challenge that is growing our restaurant business?

When it comes to mental, emotional, and financial stability, you may think that the most important is the financial aspect. After all, if you have the money to expand, the rest should just fall in place, right? If you've learnt one thing from opening your own restaurant, that should be this: having the finances in place is just half the job, the rest is all about putting out fires, mostly figurative but sometimes literal as well. Because you may be great at running a restaurant, but that doesn't automatically mean you will be great at growing and running a much larger business.

So answer these two questions honestly, and if the answer to both is a resounding "Yes", then it is time to start thinking about diving in and figuring out how you can realize your dream of expanding your successful restaurant into an even more successful chain.

There are two directions your restaurant expansion plan can take at this point: expand as a chain or start selling franchises.

If you choose to grow by starting a chain of restaurants, it means you will own every single location, and while you may hire managers to run and handle the day-to-day functioning at each location, you and only you will be ultimately responsible for every single one of the restaurants, and in turn, their profits and losses.

As a franchisor, you will sell the rights to use your restaurant's brand name, concept, method, and system of running the business, to a franchisee. And while you will provide them with the initial training and support needed, they will pretty much be on their own once they get going, paying you an initial franchise fee and ongoing royalties.

As you can see from just their definitions, there are fundamental differences between both models which means you will prefer either one or the other, and to help you decide which way forward will best suit your plans for your restaurant, I've broken down a few factors that could help you decide.

1. Capital

> Capital, needless to say, plays a huge role in helping you expand your restaurant business.
> When it comes to expanding as a chain, you will need to figure out how you're going to raise capital for every single new restaurant you open in a new

location. This means, you will need to generate capital before every single new outlet is open.

However, as a franchisor, your franchisees will pay you to allow them to use your restaurant's brand and methods, as well as use their own capital to set up the franchise.

But that doesn't mean this route is inexpensive. No route to growth really is. You not only have to deal with regulatory and compliance issues, you also need to hire staff who will run your franchise model, market your franchise, interact with and provide assistance to franchisees and much more.

2. *Complexity*

I won't say that adding another restaurant to your chain is easy, far from it. But in terms of levels of complexity, it is fairly simple. Especially when you have your first restaurant's blueprint to follow.

But starting a franchise model comes with its own complexities, many of which you may have never dealt with. You won't just have to keep your original restaurant up and running successfully to make it more attractive for new franchisees to approach you, you will also need to figure out local rules and regulations, learn how to run a franchise business, keep your franchisees happy and keep providing them with regular support such as marketing materials and ideas so they can promote their franchise. All this, as you may have guessed, isn't easy, especially if you're already knee deep in running your own restaurant and keeping it profitable.

3. *Regulation*

When it comes to a chain of restaurants, the most you will have to deal with are the usual state and local rules and regulations. If your first restaurant is in the same state, then you will already be well aware of what you need in place to make sure you comply with these.

However, franchising in many countries is regulated by a completely different body, and comes with its separate rules and regulations. There are many different aspects you will need to consider even before you start offering people a chance to be franchises, the first and most intensive of which will be your Franchise Disclosure Document—which will require you to reveal information such as your methods and complete financials.

4. *Reach*

This is actually one of the most important factors to consider before you embark on your journey of expansion. Do you want to have a branch in every city, in every state? Or do you just want to add a few more branches in your state so you can serve a much wider population? The answer to this is what will really help you choose between the two options.

If you really want to spread your restaurant and its brand far and wide, the best way forward will be the franchise model. Because managing a chain of restaurants in an area that covers the length and breadth of your country is going to be an almost impossible task. But if you have a group of franchisee locations covering the exact same area, it will not only do a great job of spreading your brand name, you won't really have to deal with as much stress and pressure either.

There are pros and cons with both, and while both are great ways to grow your restaurant business, if you can choose the option that's right for you from the start, you can rest assured that you will be on your way to running a profitable operation no matter how much it keeps growing. But if you do decide to expand into a chain of restaurants, I can help you along.

As I mentioned earlier, the best part about expanding is the fact that you can prepare for most of the eventualities that come with opening a restaurant because you're already experienced it before. The worst part is that no matter how many restaurants you have opened before, what worked for them may not always work for the one you open next. And if your first restaurant was an immense success, then growing your business without diluting your brand and credibility so you can replicate the success is a hard task that requires precise planning and perfect execution.

Does that sound intimidating? That is because it will be. But I don't just add to your worries, I also help you with tips and advice so you can work towards preparing for the unexpected and be worry-free later. So here are six aspects you should plan for, and how you can tailor your restaurant expansion strategy to give it the best chance for success.

1. Evaluate your current restaurant model

This may seem like common sense, but you won't believe the number of restaurateurs who rush into expansion without really taking into account how their current restaurant is doing.

The first thing to do, before you even start thinking about expansion, is to take stock of your current restaurant and see how successful it is, and if it is successful, whether the rate of success and the profitability it brings justifies replication. Once you're confident that your restaurant is successful and profitable, the next step is to identify the various factors that influence this profitability, and whether they can be replicated in the newer branches.

A great example of this is the current location on which your restaurant stands. Now if a major part of your success is this location, then replicating this success at other locations may not be as easy or straightforward. So make sure you take an in-depth look into every single factor that makes your restaurant a success now, to ensure every single branch you open later will be a success as well.

Another critical aspect to keep in mind is the scalability and sustainability of your restaurant model. Once your business grows to a certain size, it will be impossible for you to be hands-on everywhere, all the time. This means the restaurant should be able to function smoothly, and continue growing, without you.

2. *Figure out the finances*

Did you think that one financial plan you put together when you started your first restaurant would work for every single one you would end up opening?

Now, I will say this, because you already have proof that your restaurant concept is successful and profitable, it will open a lot more avenues for funding than you had when you were starting your first restaurant. And while all those options, such as using your own capital or taking a loan, will still be open to you, it could be less risky financially to explore other options namely investments from Venture Capitalists and Serial Investors.

As people who grow their money by investing in what could be the next big thing, if you have your finances in order and your profitability charted out, there is no reason why you would not attract investment from this avenue. Just make sure your concept is scalable, standardized and offers great quality, and you should be well on your way in terms of investment into your dream of expanding into a chain.

3. *Do your research*

Your expansion plan doesn't just depend on the success and scalability of your business concept.

Because no matter how profitable the concept has been in one market, there is no guarantee that it will be replicated in another market.

This makes market research and demographic surveys of the market you are planning on entering a must, so you can make sure you are catering to the right audience at the right place.

And it goes without saying that the location of your new restaurant also plays a huge role in your expansion plan. It is not only important to consider existing competition in the area to which you want to expand, but also make sure that it is far enough from your current branch so there is no cannibalization of potential customers between the old and new restaurant.

Location and market demographics are two of the most important aspects that will decide your future restaurant's profitability. So make sure you put in the time and effort from the start to get this right.

4. *Maintain consistency and quality*

Most people who become loyal customers to any restaurant will tell you that one of the major factors that keeps them coming back for more is consistency, both in terms of experience and quality. And this will be no different for your restaurant.

This means, while your restaurant's brand name may bring people through the door once you open your next restaurant, unless you can maintain the same consistency and quality through excellent food and service, your outlets are not going to be the success you want them to be.

A great way to ensure consistency is to standardize all the recipes that will be used in every outlet, which will ensure that the taste and quality remains the same, no matter which outlet a customer visit. Another way to offer a similar experience across your restaurants is to standardize your branding. Something as simple as the same menu design, style, and format can make all the difference in giving customers the confidence that they can expect the same quality and service from your chain of restaurants as they experienced at your original outlet.

5. *Bring in the right people*

As we've been talking about this, you must have seen that I keep mentioning how it is almost next to impossible that you will be able to be hands-on and manage every single outlet that will get added to your chain of restaurants.

This means it is crucial that you hire the right people, and give them the right training, so they can be the backbone of your new restaurant and provide the same quality and experience that you have strived to provide in your original restaurant.

After all, the success of any new outlet depends on how well it can live up the legacy of the original, and if you invest in reliable and efficient staff who you can trust to do the job right, you will be able to rest assured that no matter how many restaurants you add to your chain, they will all profitable because they are in good hands.

6. *Keep the effort going*

When you started your first restaurant, you were driven and highly motivated. But as time comes around to work towards opening your second, or even your fifth restaurant, it is possible that you will see this passion waning. And this one of the principal causes of stagnancy in restaurant chains, which ultimately leads to its failure.

It is important to remember that every restaurant in a chain plays as important a role as the next in maintaining your brand's reputation, and in turn its success and profitability. This means, making sure the same amount of effort and passion is put into every single restaurant in your chain is one of the cornerstones of the success of your restaurant expansion.

A great way to ensure this is by hiring the best management team you can at every new outlet you open, as well as using analytics and reporting to keep track of how every outlet is doing.

If you keep these areas in mind before you jump into expanding, no matter how many restaurants you add to your chain over the years, you can ensure that each is as profitable as the next, and will continue to help build your brand's name and value over the years.

Chapter 11:
The State of the Industry Today

By the time you read this, it would have been quite a long time since the WHO declared the coronavirus outbreak as a pandemic. Today the virus has spread across the globe, not just affecting the health of people, but also disrupting industries, economies, and financial markets around the world.

An industry that is especially hit by the coronavirus novel is the food & beverage industry. With quarantines enforced in some countries, and others under varying degrees of lockdown, restaurants have experienced huge losses as there is a drop in customer traffic. When many countries ordered direct closures of restaurants and bars to prevent the outbreak from spreading, they dealt a further blow to such businesses. And in this backdrop of falling footfalls, and in turn, revenues many restaurant owners are struggling to meet their expenses.

This is not even considering the growing concerns regarding complete border closures, which could drastically impact the availability of ingredients. Another huge impact is on the livelihood of the multitudes who work in the service industry and are now, effectively, unemployed until the scenario improves.

Now obviously there are restaurants and restaurant owners out there who are doing everything in their power to provide for their employees in such uncertain times.

However, most restaurants are used to working on cash flow and credit terms that usually extend to days or maybe even weeks.

But as this becomes a sustained problem they are going to have some tough decisions to make. Some restaurants are dealing with the crisis by completely flipping their business model becoming a strictly drive-through and/or delivery service.

A good work-around? Maybe.

Sustainable? Definitely not.

In the best of times, running a restaurant anywhere in the world, especially in one of the bigger cities like Dubai, New York, or London, is fraught with its own perils. High rents, low margins and an ever-growing pool of competition create a specter of terror that is always breathing down the necks of restaurant owners. But with the coronavirus pandemic, we are all in an uncharted territory.

Even in countries where the quarantine rules have been relaxed, the situation is not much better. And the reason for this is multi-fold.

First, even though lockdowns have been lifted, the uncertainty and fear caused by the virus still remain. In the current scenario, people prefer to be at home and avail of deliveries and take away so as to reduce their social interactions. And even when customers do decide to dine in at a restaurant, it is more often to celebrate an occasion than just a random night out with friends and family.

Second, restaurants themselves have had to reduce the number of tables they have on their premises so as to comply with social distancing norms. This in turn automatically affects their bottom line as they can now only serve a limited number of customers at any point of time. Additionally, they've also had to cut down on staff as well. Both the front and back of the house teams have been reduced drastically. Most of the employees who have been retained are those who can multitask and offer more in different job roles than for the one they have been retained. The big guns who pulled heavy salaries are being put under the spotlight, and time and effort is now being spent to find the right people, with processes and measures being put together to keep the business afloat.

Third, many restaurants, especially in Dubai, had become used to offering average meal and beverage options for exorbitant prices. However, with people now choosing to dine out sparingly, such restaurants need to up their game as such as offering is no longer going to cut it. In fact, this period of lockdown has had the most impact on fine dining restaurants because people are now looking for more value for money. And with the current scenario, it doesn't seem like this sphere of dining is going to improve interest and earnings for the next couple of years.

However, it is not all doom and gloom. Restaurants that will survive this onslaught on their business are those whose owners take the necessary steps to keep their business agile and evolving. A great example is that of Noma, who are now planning on opening a burger chain for the time being as they deal with losing customers for their fine dining offering. People have also been taking pay cuts for the time being to help the businesses they work at recover and have a better chance of surviving in the long run. And as you can possibly see around you if you live in a city where the lockdown has been lifted, many restaurants are back to doing a good amount of business. It may be not how they used to run things pre-lockdown, but by evolving and changing to fit today's scenario, they have managed to stay afloat.

This means if you can take the necessary steps to keep your restaurant and its offerings relevant in today's times, and you hire right, you can ride the storm that is this pandemic and come out the other end reasonably unscathed.

Chapter 12:
Some final words

As I part ways with you, I can't think of anything better to share than my graduation speech that I gave when I graduated from OCLD. I hope this will inspire you to go out there and achieve your dreams, just as I have done.

A rich man once threw a pool side party and once all his guests had gathered, he made this rather bizarre announcement – If anyone can jump into the swimming pool and swim from one end to another I will give him a million bucks!!! Sounded simple enough but the rich man revealed to everyone's shock and horror that the pool was full of hungry and dangerous alligators. No sooner had he made the announcement, that a young guest jumped in and swam with all his energy from one end to another in express time and as he emerged from the pool, the rich man walked up to him and said – Congratulations, you just won yourself a million bucks, now how do you want to be paid – cash, cheque or bank transfer. The young guest gathering his breath and barely managing to speak said – I don't want any money!!! All I want to know is just WHO PUSHED ME IN????

Good morning parents, teachers, honored guests and soon to be graduates. On 16th of July 2011, I Nigel Lobo walked into this sprawling campus thinking precisely the same thing – just who pushed me in. Some of us got here out of choice, some compulsion and some I dare say confusion from varied paths of life, from colleges of international and national repute. With rapidly beating hearts and nervous minds we entered the Institution known as one of the best institutions for Hotel Management training in India – the OCLD .

And today, 19th June 2013, we have come together to celebrate a turning point in the lives of the remarkable and amazing group of people standing before me. We have learned, laughed, loved, gotten into trouble, and most of all matured together. But the moment to venture on our own into the "real world" and truly pursue our passions has finally come. With greater confidence, knowledge and awareness of the world, we are about to cross the final line.

In thinking about what I wanted to say to you today, I asked several of my graduating friends what words of wisdom I could impart today and it came to sound something like this:

No. 1: Don't Screw up!
No. 2: Be Funny

Obviously after these two gems of advice, I am prepared with a stunning and powerful speech that will remain with every one of us till the day we die. Or at least until one of the real speakers comes up here and says something meaningful. It's hard to believe that we'll all be leaving this place finally. It is even harder to believe that from now on, we're going to pretty much have to fend for ourselves.

OCLD is not just a school; it is a way of life; a spirit that animates daily your life with the spirit of teamwork, the spirit of solidarity and the spirit of service. Together we have supported each other through long days of scraping and serving water, we learned how to carry more than 3 plates at once and how to balance a glass on a round tray without dropping it down someone's back. Together we have survived long hours in the kitchen with Chef NAME breathing down our necks and we have learned how to appreciate a nice NAME A DISH FOR WHICH TASTE HAS TO BE DEVELOPED.

The most common answer I got when I asked my fellow graduates what OCLD has meant to them was; amazing friends, and I believe that this is one of the reasons why OCLD will always have a special place in our hearts.

Just the mere mention of OCLD brings back so many memories, nostalgia that threatens to pour out in tears. All those grueling language exams, viva and sessions where I barely managed to keep my eyes open. Those blissful hours spent in the library, lazing around in the lounge.

In these years, we met strangers who became our best friends, we met teachers who became our mentors, we met colleagues who became our teachers. Those private secret conversations we shared with our friends. The relationships we made. The relationships we broke.

To all our seniors who cared so much for our WELFARE but for whom we could not even give a FAREWELL!

To the junior batch for hosting such a wonderful evening. You all made the impossible happen tonight. I am pretty sure you're also glad to see the back of us.

May your Supervisory and Executive Stages treat you well and may you get kind managers to shadow.

To each of my own batch mates for being extremely cool and being so forgiving towards my painful attitude. To those I hurt, today I say sorry.

To our parents – yes Dad, yes Mom, we are here thanks to you. You make this all worth it!

To my fellow graduates, we all come from different walks of life, we all have different stories to tell about our journey to OCLD, and after today we will all embark on unique paths. Yet, the common thread that runs among us is the desire for a brighter future and despite our individualized views about what that future may look like, we chose OCLD to bring us one step closer to our ultimate goal, to give us the tools we need for a better future, or simply to give us a new beginning. And what we got in return was perhaps more than we ever expected—we have each found a home here at OCLD, one filled with supportive and caring teachers, administration and staff.

I was once told that you're only as good as the people that you surround yourself with. Well, there is not a higher caliber of people that I would rather surround myself with than you all sitting in front of me today. We often don't realize the contribution to our growth our faculty has made but undeniably they are worthy of high praise. This Institute would be nothing but a Structure of walls & pillars with beautiful infrastructure & greenery, if it weren't for our World class, fantastic and awesome faculty. They are the true spirit of The Oberoi group, people who have dedicated their lives to this Institute making it what it is, and making us what we are. Of course we must never forget the Office staff & non-teaching staff who have always been very cooperative and helpful in shaping us.

As we close this chapter and continue to write the pages of our lives, let's never forget the bridges we've crossed, the bonds we've shared and the memories that we've made and when we all come back and see each other again for our 20-year reunion, there are going to be all sorts of surprises. By that time NAME A COLLEAGUE will probably be FILL IN THE BLANKS, NAME ANOTHER COLLEAGUE will be the new reigning arm wrestling champion of the world / or something similar (funny). NAME ANOTHER COLLEAGUE will have his very own morning talk show called "Wake up with a cup of NAME", NAME ANOTHER COLLEAGUE (can be a teacher / admin staff) will be the FILL IN THE BLANKS, NAME ONE LAST COLLEAGUE (someone cute and clumsy) will be... well, let's be honest, there really isn't much hope for NAME THAT PERSON, (turn to that person) – NAME I guess you should have just tried a little harder... FILL IN THE BLANKS.

Let's always remember the important role that OCLD played in helping us accomplish some of our many goals. Remember that some of the greater things in life are unseen; that's why you close your eyes when you kiss, cry, or dream.

If you don't remember a single word of what I've said up here today, just remember this: Jobs, houses, money, and success will all come and go, but the one thing that nobody can ever take away from you are the good times and good friends you have had here at OCLD.

My fellow graduates, right at this moment in your life, you are in a unique position that you may never ever be in again. You have nothing to lose. Everything you have acquired of value is locked inside you. If you have a dream, now is the time to pursue it. It is all up to you.

So, in closing, I only have one more thing to say. I consider today to be a defining milestone in a very long and blessed journey and I am proud to say that I am a part of the OCLD batch of 2013.

Congratulations, goodbye and God bless.